ADVANCE PRAISE FOR

Women, Violence, & Testimony in the Works of Zora Neale Hurston

"Diana Miles argues that Zora Neale Hurston's works are trauma testimonies in which she revisits repeatedly the sites of pain and suffering, especially domestic violence, that occurred in her own life and in the lives of her family members, particularly her parents. Through creatively delineating trauma, Hurston transforms her own experience and vies for witnesses who will find in her works strategies for comparable transformation.... Miles persuasively argues that Hurston's individualized approach to a creativity saturated with trauma testimony effectively moves her beyond limitations of race, gender, and class and into more universalized psychological encounters with readers at the points where all human experience intersects. Miles's book will assuredly inspire re-evaluation of Hurston's novels, autobiography, and aesthetic, as well as previous criticism of her work. It also has the potential to inspire psychoanalytic considerations of other African American authors and works about whom critical commentary is too frequently steeped exclusively in the racial vat."

Trudier Harris, J. Carlyle Sitterson Professor of English,
The University of North Carolina at Chapel Hill

"In this work, Diana Miles moves beyond the celebration of authentic folk language so often the focus of Hurston criticism and takes a closer look at the implications of the violent content which also characterizes Hurston's work. In a book supported convincingly by trauma theorists, Miles examines Hurston's novels and autobiography as testimonial sites of the domestic violence and racial oppression experienced by many black women during the late nineteenth and early twentieth centuries. By offering testimony to this trauma in her works, Hurston allows her readers to 'bear witness' to the stories of the victims and thus set in motion a necessary part of the healing process. Miles offers a careful, insightful, and long overdue analysis of Hurston's work. You will want to read Hurston—and many other writers whose testimonies of trauma we may have missed—all over again after reading this book."

Carolyn C. Denard, Department of English,
Georgia State University

Women, Violence, & Testimony
in the Works
of Zora Neale Hurston

AFRICAN AMERICAN LITERATURE AND CULTURE

EXPANDING AND EXPLODING THE BOUNDARIES

Carlyle V. Thompson
General Editor

Vol. 3

PETER LANG
New York • Washington, D.C./Baltimore • Bern
Frankfurt am Main • Berlin • Brussels • Vienna • Oxford

Diana Miles

Women, Violence, & Testimony in the Works of Zora Neale Hurston

PETER LANG
New York • Washington, D.C./Baltimore • Bern
Frankfurt am Main • Berlin • Brussels • Vienna • Oxford

Library of Congress Cataloging-in-Publication Data

Miles, Diana.
Women, violence, and testimony in the works of Zora Neale Hurston / Diana Miles.
p. cm. — (African-American literature and culture; vol. 3)
Includes bibliographical references and index.
1. Hurston, Zora Neale—Characters—Women. 2. Feminism and literature—
United States—History—20th century. 3. Women and literature—United States—
History—20th century. 4. Feminist fiction, American—History and criticism.
5. African American women in literature. 6. Psychic trauma in literature. 7. Witnesses
in literature. 8. Violence in literature. 9. Women in literature. I. Title. II. Series.
PS3515.U789 Z7855   813'.52—dc21   2001038782
ISBN 0-8204-5751-5
ISSN 1528-3887

Die Deutsche Bibliothek-CIP-Einheitsaufnahme

Miles, Diana:
Women, violence, and testimony in the works of Zora Neale Hurston / Diana Miles.
—New York; Washington, D.C./Baltimore; Bern;
Frankfurt am Main; Berlin; Brussels; Vienna; Oxford: Lang.
(African-American literature and culture; Vol. 3)
ISBN 0-8204-5751-5

Cover design by Joni Holst

The paper in this book meets the guidelines for permanence and durability
of the Committee on Production Guidelines for Book Longevity
of the Council of Library Resources.

© 2003 Peter Lang Publishing, Inc., New York
275 Seventh Avenue, 28th Floor, New York, NY 10001
www.peterlangusa.com

Printed in the United States of America

To Vareck Lanier Gober Sr. and Jr.

Together you echo the rhythms of my heart . . .
bone of my bone, flesh of my flesh.

Contents

Acknowledgments

The completion of this study would not have been possible without the enduring patience and care of my family, friends, and mentors. Specifically I would like to thank my father, George R. Davis Jr., and mother, Donna Davis, for their constant support. I would not have been able to accomplish this work without my husband, who made sure I ate and rested, or without my son, Vareck Jr., who carried countless books through libraries for me. I thank my brother, Dewey, for his abiding faith and encouragement. I am eternally grateful to Linda Sampson Danavall, who once saved my life and Zoe Lattimer, who has been a model of great courage for me. I am also indebted to the strengthening spirits of Frances Miles Dickson and Dewey Miles Sr., may they rest in peace.

I also extend my deepest gratitude to my writing partners, Patricia King and Anna Engle. Even though we worked on different projects, we wrote in the same house, and I was surprisingly sustained by the sound of our thirty fingers furiously typing away. A special note of appreciation goes to my dear friend Michael Antonnucci, whose careful reading of every draft helped to shape this project.

I would also like to thank those who mentored me at Emory University. In many different ways, each of these individuals affirmed my work and provided direction. I thank Mark A. Sanders for his constant patience and support. I am grateful to Cathy Caruth for her brilliant work and her guidance. I am also grateful to Walter Kaladjian for his sound advice and his willingness to listen. I thank Frances Smith Foster for her sincere interest in my well-being. At the end of this process, I am honored to be able to call Randall K. Burkett my friend. I will never forget Richard Long's willingness to assist me with my research, and I thank Rudolph Byrd for his direction when I needed it. I am also deeply indebted to Gerri Moreland, Melanie Tipnis, Andrea de Man, and Jackie Ally, who made sure that I met my deadlines.

Without the support of the highly attentive staff in Special Collections at Florida State University, the Moorland Spingarn Research Center at Howard University, and the Library of Congress, or Victoria Sanders, literary agent for the Zora Neale Hurston estate, and editor, Heidi Burns, this work would not be possible. I thank you all.

Finally, I reserve my deepest gratitude for God, whose hand rests firmly on my life.

DFM

Introduction

Zora Neale Hurston was born on January 15, 1891, in Notasulga, Alabama. By 1892, her family had moved to the all-black town of Eatonville, Florida, where she was raised.[1] Hurston's many journeys away from her Eatonville home led her to produce a body of testimonial literature that is anthropological, historical, and extremely personal. Her works critique cultural responses to the complex race, class, and gender constructions that shaped her own rural community. While a vast amount of Hurston scholarship discusses Hurston's treatment of these issues, this project aims to expand the discussion by reading Hurston's first two novels, *Jonah's Gourd Vine* (1934) and *Their Eyes Were Watching God* (1937), and her autobiography, *Dust Tracks on a Road* (1942), as testimonial literature.

A biographically based, testimonial reading of Hurston's work addresses her persistent return to the themes of death and violence. Trauma testimony expresses, among other things, the survivor's repetitive return to events that are not fully known or understood at the moment they occur because they are too overwhelming to fully comprehend. Traumatic events shock the consciousness, and therefore, in varying degrees, these events are not psychically or emotionally integrated. The survivor's repetitive return is his or her attempt to revisit and revise the lost moment, thereby integrating it into the consciousness. As a product of creativity, and because of its indirectness, testimonial literature epitomizes the paradoxical nature of all testimonial projects: The act of telling or giving testimony is inherently linked to silence around the event(s). Testimony should be read creatively because it is not direct. In fact, testimony is linked to the silence of not knowing that occurs with traumatic events. In other words, the imperative to tell one's own story of trauma is, in part, born out of a desire to translate into language an experience that is, initially, too overwhelming for the survivor to fully comprehend: "The emergence of the narrative, which is being listened to and heard is therefore the process and the place wherein cognizance, the 'knowing' of the event is given birth to."[2] In Hurston's case, a testimonial reading of her work addresses her persistent returns to the violence and oppression experienced by black women in her rural community. Hurston's publication dates span from the 1920s to the 1950s, and some of her most renowned works are among the earliest critiques, by a modern American writer, of violence against women.

Even though the American reform campaign against domestic violence dates back to the temperance crusade of the 1840s, until the 1960s there was very little progress toward ending the practice of violence against women. There was "[v]irtually no public discussion of wife beating from the turn of the century until the mid-1970s. Wife beating was called 'domestic disturbance' by the police [and] 'family maladjustment' by marriage counselors and social caseworkers. Psychiatry, under the influence of Helen Deutsch, regarded the battered woman as a masochist who provoked her husband into beating her. In the *Journal of Marriage and the Family,* the major scholarly journal in family sociology, no article on family violence appeared from its founding in 1930 until 1969."[3]

Public attention to family violence and a heightened public sensitivity to the discriminatory and abusive nature of sexism in American culture was the direct result of feminist movements of the 1960s and 1970s. However, the issue of race hindered the progress toward making domestic violence a crime against *all* women: "When the first anthologies of sexual abuse survivor testimony appeared, narratives by women of color were ignored, decontextualized, or appropriated. Although this was arguably not the intent of anthologizers, their exclusion of women of color as speaking voices served to reinscribe patterns of discrimination already in the culture."[4] Hurston's bold attempts to address these issues approximately thirty-five years earlier underscore her commitment to improving social conditions for women.

Hurston repeatedly produced narratives that discuss, in varying degrees, domestic violence. Her first novel, *Jonah's Gourd Vine,* introduces readers to domestic violence from the very start. Her most acclaimed novel, *Their Eyes Were Watching God,* presents directly and indirectly numerous acts of violence against women, and her autobiography, *Dust Tracks on a Road,* testifies to her own personal experiences with violence. However, only a sparse amount of criticism directly addresses the violence against women in her work.[5] Critical silence around violence against women is due, in part, to the lingering taboo that considers the negative portrayal of black men, by the African American community, as a type of treason.

Beth E. Richie, author of "Battered Black Women: A Challenge for the Black Community," attests to the survival of this taboo into the late twentieth century. Richie's work in the black and Hispanic communities of New York revealed that "the political machine at the forefront of the grassroots community movement was, in fact, subtly exploiting women by denying the reality of sexual oppression. . . .

[This she calls] the trap of silence. . . . [As a black woman, she] was immobilized by denial and sadness. Fear of being cast out of the community silenced [her], in the beginning. Loyalty and devotion are enormous barriers to overcome."[6]

Richie contacted a group called Battered Minority Women (BMW) and found them articulating a belief that demanded silence as [an] initial response to violence against black women. BMW explained, "black women are beaten solely because their men are deprived. . . . Black women should involve themselves in the struggle for racial justice in order to end battering in their own homes . . . responsibility lies with white society."[7] The relationship between supporting the struggle for racial justice and keeping silent about injustice within the African community is a historically gendered relationship, rooted in the racial uplift movements of the late nineteenth and early twentieth centuries. While uplift ideology is a broad term with debatable definitions, one of the dominant approaches to racial uplift during this era greatly restricted women: "Gender conflict exposed the contradictions of uplift's vision of progress, [which was] a middle-class vision structured in sexual dominance."[8]

Another reason for the critical silence around the rampant violence in Hurston's work is that our ability to identify literature of trauma is relatively recent. Not until the 1920 publication of Sigmund Freud's *Beyond the Pleasure Principle* were we given a foundation for the analysis of trauma testimony that appears in literary form.[9] In *Beyond,* Freud posits the notion of traumatic repetition, which describes the very structure of trauma itself. He defines the circumstances of trauma as limited to a psychically unprepared encounter with danger.[10] As a result, he notes that survivors exhibit a repetition compulsion manifesting as a return to "the situation of [the] accident."[11] Freud explains the psychological purpose of repetition through his description of a little boy's game that reenacts the trauma of his mother's departure with the added dimension of her pleasurable return. The boy's staging of her pleasurable return gives insight into the repetitive returns to the trauma of her departure. Initially, Freud thought that "her departure had to be enacted as a necessary preliminary to her joyful return, and it was in the latter that lay the true purpose of the game."[12] Ultimately, he rejects the pleasurable aspect of this game for a much more insightful explanation. He posits the notion that survivors, like children, revisit the event to "make themselves master of the situation" that they were unprepared for in reality.[13]

By drawing attention to survivors' repetitive return to trauma as a means of mastery or gaining control at a specific point in time when there was none, Freud leads us to think critically about the very nature of artistic production and its possible relationship to trauma and repetition. After noting that artistic reenactments of painful experiences carried out by adults could be enjoyable for them, he became convinced that "there are ways and means enough of making what is in itself unpleasurable into a subject to be worked over in the mind."[14] Freud recommends that a discussion of artistic reenactments of painful experiences and the analysis of traumatic repetition where pleasure is the outcome "should be undertaken by some system of aesthetics."[15]

Critical analysis of Hurston's artistic reenactments of trauma leads me to further suggest that the interpretive dimension of psychoanalysis and the discursive quality of aesthetic production can be understood as working together toward psychic resolution. That this resolution may never be completely realized is irrelevant. What is relevant is that the process of repetition and revision provides a framework for the survivor to attempt to master psychically rupturing events. In addition, the very nature of the creative process, which is fraught with repetition and revision, makes it suitable for honoring the survivor's imperative to bear witness to others.

Since Freud's 1920 publication, psychoanalytic theorists, literary scholars, and political activists continue to work toward learning how to understand the repetitive aspect of testimony. Part of this work includes fulfilling what Freud alluded to in *Beyond* as the audience's role, or the ethical role of secondary witnessing.[16] In his 1994 essay, "Jean Améry as Witness," Alvin Rosenfeld defines the role of the secondary witness to act as "witness for the witnesses. . . . [T]hey have a crucial role to play in the literature of testimony. They 'complete' the historical and testimonial record by a complementary act that helps to fulfill . . . [the] aim to 're-member the past in the future.'"[17] Rosenfeld's essay provides us with a view of "victimage as [having] an emphatic moral value and that the only way to understand this [moral value] is to keep alive its memory in terms that stress its scandalous character: 'The moral person demands annulment of time—in the case under question, by nailing the criminal to his deed. Thereby, . . . the latter can join his victim as a fellow human being.'"[18] I suggest that as readers of testimony, we must reconsider literary depictions of experience, history, and identity as quite often bound to the moral demands of the author. Esther Rashkin's *Family Secrets and the Psychoanalysis of Narrative* "identif[ies] visible elements of selected narratives as symptoms or 'symbols' that point to unspeakable family dramas cryptically inscribed within them."[19] Her project reflects an effort of recovery that is vital to the project of locating trauma narratives misunderstood as works that are *primarily* motivated and organized around the imaginative impulses of the writers.

In her essay, "The Phalaris Syndrome: Alain Robbe-Grillet vs. D. M. Thomas," K. J. Phillips explores the reasons why these texts are misunderstood. She argues that we "inherit our modern problems of reading violence from specific practices of allegory and abstraction that started to come into vogue in the late 18th century and have continued into the 20th." She goes on to reject the popular notion that the "writer must 'express a world view' or must 'recount a preconceived story' . . . [since this notion] fail[s] to perceive that the modern training not to notice violence as it disappears into allegory or literary pattern might itself be a worldview."[20] The growing interest in psychoanalytic readings of literature resists the tendency "not [to] notice violence." Instead, psychoanalytic readings of testimonial literature provide us with the opportunity to examine our cultural reception of violence and the ways in which testimony can empower or paralyze us.

The leading scholars of trauma testimony teach us to trace the structure of trauma and to observe its formal qualities as a way of identifying the sites where writers weave fiction and testimony together in the attempt to form a coherent narrative of self and the world. Cathy Caruth's groundbreaking text, *Unclaimed Experience: Trauma, Narrative, and History*, examines the wide range of genres that constitute sites of testimony. She places her discussion of Freud's *Moses and Monotheism* alongside Marguerite Duras's *Hiroshima Mon Amour* and introduces her text by expanding on Freud's concept of traumatic neurosis with an apt description of the "literary resonance . . . the enigma of the otherness of a human voice that cries out from the wound."[21] A similar mix of genres occurs in Kali Tal's *Worlds of Hurt*, which opens with an insightful chapter titled "Worlds of Hurt: Reading Literatures of Trauma" followed by Vietnam War narratives and the testimony of incest survivors. Deirdre Lashgari's carefully edited *Violence, Silence, and Anger: Women's Writing as Transgression* also includes a wide range of narratives addressing women's positions in relation to the violence of war, rape, and slavery. As a result, Lashgari's text contributes to our understanding of the ways that cultural relations inform acts of testimony.[22] The works of these scholars ask us to attend to issues of voicelessness by providing a way of hearing women, veterans, Jewish Holocaust survivors, and other survivors of violence. Attending to these issues requires the deliberate positioning of oneself in an ethical relation to the survivor and to his or her act of testimony.

It is important to note that testimony has an address, and when the testimony appears in the form of a published text, it is addressed to the world. The narrative becomes not just the story of one "individual in relation to the events of his own past; instead, it is the story of the way in which one's own trauma is tied up with the trauma of another, the way in which trauma may lead, therefore, to the encounter with another, through the very possibility and surprise of listening to another's wound."[23] All testimony requires an audience of ethical listeners who will not only receive the narrative but will also act upon the ethical demand behind the testimony, which is to ensure that the traumatic event will not occur again.

The chapters that follow are developed, in part, by using the insights offered by a wide range of trauma theorists whose works reflect a desire to aid survivors in establishing a community of secondary witnesses. While I have no intention of conflating the varied theoretical schools of thought, I am also not interested in engaging in a debate over whether or not a particular trend of thought is more or less valid in its analysis of trauma testimony. There are, as Caruth points out, differing trends in the approach to analyzing trauma testimony. Some believe that the experience of trauma results in the complete shattering of the former self. Others argue that it results in a psychic numbing. There are those, like Tal, who engage in a deconstruction of the theorist as a way of authenticating the theory. These debates and others like them do nothing to further my particular project. In fact, the variety of theoretical approaches to understanding trauma testimony help establish the commonality of human responses to trauma.

The broad use of a variety of theorists from differing schools of thought ideologically helps my project, which is to offer a psychological analysis of the works of a black, female artist whose worldviews have been previously explained within the contexts of race, gender, and/or sociology. By emphasizing the generally agreed-upon symptoms of trauma and the frame of testimony, I am able to locate the testimonial aspects of Zora Neale Hurston's works. Also, in a much broader context, I call into question the nature of the relationship between race, class, and gender constructs, and the experience of psychic trauma.

Because these socially constructed identities facilitate and sanction physical violence and other forms of trauma, they are defined here as the tools of social control. These constructs are often referenced by perpetrators prior to and during various acts of dehumanization and alienation. I suggest, however, that it is not the race, class, or gender constructs that traumatize, but rather, the dehumanization of one human being by another. For example, an African American slave woman who has had her child sold away is traumatized by the loss of her child and the loss of her freedom, not her blackness. Likewise, a raped woman is traumatized by the violent attack, not her womanhood. The distinction is important because as individuals attempt to give testimony and gain *a sense of mastery* over their traumas, they must be able to clearly locate the source of psychic rupture. Survivors are also better equipped to reenter their communities if they do not relinquish *the sustaining aspects* of their race, gender, and class realities.

The powerful relationship between individual trauma survivors and their communities is clear when we examine how "the constant presence and threat of trauma in the lives of girls and women of all colors, men of color in the United States, [and] lesbian and gay people has shaped our society."[24] "What does it mean if we admit that our culture is a factory for the production of so many walking wounded? What is the effect on members of our society when the mere threat of trauma is as effective as an actual traumatic incident because of its foundation in historical reality? One result of a lifetime risk of exposure to certain trauma is that "[p]ost-traumatic symptoms can be[come] intergenerational . . . [and] can be spread laterally throughout an oppressed social group."[25] The generational transmission of posttraumatic symptoms within the debilitating constructs of race, class, and gender diverts attention away from the actual causes of trauma—psychic unpreparedness for a life-threatening or dehumanizing experience. This diversion hinders the process of healing for all; in vain, survivors and their communities legislatively treat the issues of race, class, and gender as if these constructs were in-and-of-themselves traumatic.

By avoiding debates concerning the Jewishness of the Holocaust, the blackness of American slavery, or the primacy of a symbolic reference to trauma versus a figurative reference, I am able to draw overarching conclusions about the psychic effects of traumatic experience and the relationship between all survivors and their communities. I am able to demonstrate that while religion, race, class, gender, region, and nation can be, and often are, socially constructed to enable the occurrence of violence that causes traumatic experiences, the psychic processing of trauma is a human process.

Because she is black, female, and from a rural community, Hurston is an ideal candidate for this examination. In spite of her many socially constructed identities, her psychological response to the traumas of her life shares the repetitive returns, psychic splitting, and temporality of many other survivors from different races, classes, eras, and genders. Testimonies of Jewish Holocaust survivors, Vietnam Veterans, and rape survivors were equally useful to this project because of these similarities. Whether the survivor came out of 1972 Southeast Asia, or 1941 Germany, or a small rural Alabama town in the 1880s, all of their testimonies constitute "human documents rather than merely historical ones, [and they] reflect the troubled interaction between past and present."[26] While many of the theorists whose work I use are from differing theoretical schools, they are in general agreement concerning the following aspects of trauma: Numerous conditions can produce psychic trauma; the testimonial process that occurs between survivor and secondary witness is crucial to establishing the survivor's role in the community; there is a close relationship between the survivor's repetition of trauma and the transmission of intergenerational trauma, and there is a consistent manifestation of psychic self-division and latency associated with trauma.

My use of a variety of theorists to locate the consistencies of human responses to trauma survival will, I hope, disrupt the tendency of human groups to claim propriety over loss and suffering. While I rely most heavily on Cathy Caruth's *Unclaimed Experience* (1996) and her edited collection of essays, *Trauma: Explorations in Memory* (1995), I also refer to the findings of Sigmund Freud, Dori Laub, Judith Herman, Shoshana Felman, Kali Tal, Lawrence Langer, and others. I hope that the broad use of a variety of theorists will help to underscore the ways in which "the material realities of a runaway slave woman desperate to save her child have much to say to those of a Jewish mother in a concentration camp. So, too, do the injunctions to remember both survival and loss, whether they are directed towards a black adult incest survivor or a white adolescent girl."[27] Because her texts provide the framework for an analysis of the many forms of testimony within the African American community and how they are received, Hurston acts as both griot and healer. As a result, her work should be understood, primarily, as an injunction to remember history and loss.

As trauma survivors attempt to reestablish relationships within their communities, community members are placed in an ethical relationship with survivors. By receiving testimony, the entire community becomes a body made up of secondary witnesses who are vital to the process of reintegrating the survivor into the community. Forging this ethical relationship through testimony establishes a matrix of experience wherein the individual traumatic experience is also the community's traumatic experience. We see the result of this most clearly through the testimonial acts by survivors of the Jewish Holocaust. An examination of how recipients of trauma testimony silence, ignore, or reshape survivor narratives reveals a great deal about the social patterns that shape our society. The exchange of testimony between individuals and their immediate family, the family and the surrounding community, and finally, the community's exchange of testimony with the nation tell a great deal about how we value each other.[28] By using Hurston's work to examine the relationship between testimony and secondary witness, I hope to offer insight that will help explain why cultural wounds that should have begun to heal in 1865 continue to cause pain in the United States in the twenty-first century.[29]

America lays claim to a national literature that represents the historical experiences of the individual, the community, and the nation. We have deconstructed, analyzed, reconstructed, and then categorized our literature so that we can call upon it to help us make sense of ourselves. Some of the general categorizations include political, economical, ethnic, religious, and feminist texts, and they are read and understood as centrally motivated by the need to comment on or reform one or another of our social systems. As a result, we find trauma narratives within various categories such as captivity narratives, slave narratives, narratives of racial uplift, and historical narratives. Only recently have literary critics begun to examine the organizing power of trauma and to investigate how trauma dictates the form and language of testimonial narratives. Shoshana Felman contributes to this examination by discussing the act of testimony. She begins by explaining that what

> testimony does not offer [is] a completed statement, a totalizable account of . . . events. In testimony, language is in process and in trial; it does not possess itself as a conclusion, as the contestation of a verdict or the self-transparency of knowledge. Testimony is, in other words, a discursive *practice,* as opposed to a pure *theory.* To testify—to *vow to tell,* to *promise* and *produce* one's own speech as material evidence for truth—is to accomplish a *speech act,* rather than to simply formulate a statement.[30]

Kali Tal's continuation of this discussion explains that the language of testimony refuses to offer a singular and completed statement since it is invested with "multiple meanings encoded in particular 'loaded' signifiers *(blood, terror, murder)* [which] characterize survivor writing, and distinguish it from other genres."[31] These recent critical works expand the genre of survivor writing by requiring that many texts be reread and newly discovered.

Zora Neale Hurston's position as a survivor of personal and historical trauma calls for a rereading of her work that acknowledges the influence of her personal chaos. I will discuss *Jonah's Gourd Vine, Their Eyes Were Watching God,* and *Dust Tracks on a Road* as three parts of a singular testimony that is both personal and communal. These three texts are particularly important because together they constitute a detailed autobiographical narrative of her family history and the impact it had on her. *Jonah's Gourd Vine* gives a full account of Hurston's perspective on the violently enforced power dynamics at work in her parents' marriage. *Their Eyes Were Watching God* continues her narrative by presenting a persona of herself in the form of the protagonist, Janie. Through this persona, Hurston explores her own violent relationship and ultimately offers a female character whose ability to reproduce is independent of her violent heterosexual relationships. *Dust Tracks on a Road* is, paradoxically, her actual autobiography and stands as the most deliberately self-constructed figuration of Hurston to date.

In certain sections of Hurston's autobiography, she deliberately delivers a superhuman image of invincibility. I read these sections as constructed identities that demonstrate her attempt to master the traumas of her life. However, the section describing her mother's death, and her response to the event, along with the sections describing her familial relationships are understood as testimony to factual events. Hurston's biographer, Robert Hemenway, verifies the actual occurrence of these events, and her repetitive, literary returns to these events underscore their powerful impact on her life. I would argue that all three texts are linked by Hurston's persistent drive to revisit and revise personal trauma. Because each text represents a new attempt to give testimony to a different aspect of her experience, they are read on a continuum.[32]

One of Hurston's earliest published pieces was the short story "Spunk," which won the 1925 *Opportunity* writers' contest.[33] From the start, she was heralded for her ability to make art out of her rural Eatonville experiences. Critics overlooked the thematic content of her work and focused, instead, on the quaint rural images and her use of language and folklore. It is important to note that in the cultural context of rural Eatonville, one can only tell well-embellished tales from a position of authority. While many critics have acknowledged Hurston's authority to speak for her own community, few have noted the impact that her testimonial process had on the production of her texts. Because writing is also an act of testimony for Hurston, her narratives rely on both ethnographic and autobiographical material as a resource for the testimony of silenced women in her community and in her family.

Critics are only beginning to understand the testimonial function of literary expression; consequently, Hurston's use of ethnography, dialect, and autobiography has not always been well received. In his 1972 introduction to *Jonah's Gourd Vine*, Larry Neal finds that "the central achievement of [this novel] is Zora Neale Hurston's success in penetrating the 'romantic' surface of rural, black Southern life . . . despite her tendency to overwork her dialect, to render it with such phonetic faithfulness that some of the real poetry embedded in black speech either is obscured or goes unexploited."[34] Similarly, when discussing *Jonah's Gourd Vine* in her 1993 essay, "Changing Her Own Words," Cheryl Wall finds that "too often folklore overwhelms the formal narrative."[35] In her 1934 article "Characteristics of Negro Expression," Hurston calls this expressive tendency "the will to adorn," and states that this very tendency is the foundation of African American folklore, which orally transmits survival techniques in the form of short stories.[36] By combining elements of the folkloric tradition with her own personal history, Hurston develops a novel that examines the violence of her own family and communal history.

The most challenging aspect of examining testimony within fiction is separating historical fact from fiction in the attempt to hear the actual testimony: "The issue of how memory and history become art is always a complicated one; . . . [in certain cases] the question is also whether they *should* become art."[37] In the case of African American fiction, where fictionalized settings frame responses to or depictions of historical reality, memory and history are both apt resources for artistic expression. This is especially true in the case of Hurston, whose training as an anthropologist underscores the factual elements of her work. Historically, the African American literary canon emerged as a response to the accusation that African Americans "lacked a formal and collective history. . . . The narrated, descriptive 'eye' was put into service as a literary form to posit both the individual 'I' of the black author as well as the collective 'I' of the race."[38] Therefore, Hurston's use of folklore and the dialect necessary to its proper telling is appropriate for the act of testimony to individual and collective history.

The overlapping histories of the personal and the collective constitute the foundation of the African American literary tradition from which Hurston emerges. This "tradition . . . rests on the framework built . . . by the first-person narratives of black ex-slaves" whose pleas very often overshadowed the force of their protest.[39] The antebellum testimonial narrative typically required authentication from a white witness and careful editing from white abolitionists. Slave narratives served to reveal the inhumanity of slavery and gain support for the abolition movement. The antebellum slave narrative developed a tradition that nourished the works of Booker T. Washington, Malcolm X, Ralph Ellison, Richard Wright, Ishmael Reed, Octavia Butler, and Toni Morrison, to name a few. However, as Claudia Tate explains in *Psychoanalysis and Black Novels,* audiences

> have typically associated the explicit discourses of a work with its stated social themes, while attributing the applied meaning inscribed in its rhetorical strategies to its aesthetic design rather than to its conceptual propositions. Such a separation of form and content

has been particularly troublesome in African American literature because it has produced a reception history marked by the color line. Black reviewers have generally applauded those works by African Americans that emphatically focus on the political aspirations of racial equality. And white reviewers tended to applaud those corresponding works that concentrate on their aesthetic development.[40]

These critical tendencies appear in the *New Masses* 1941 review of *Their Eyes Were Watching God* by Ralph Ellison; he accuses her of writing another "calculated burlesque show" and setting her story in an all-black town rather than in a realistic setting where the South's brutalities might "intrude."[41] Conversely, in his 1935 review of *Jonah's Gourd Vine*, a white reviewer, H. I. Brock of the *New York Times,* gives a round of applause to the

> tall tales rich with flavor and alive with characteristic turns of speech. Those of us who have known the Southern Negro from our youth find him here speaking the language of his tribe as familiarly as if it came straight out of his own mouth and had not been translated into type and transmitted through the eye to the ear. Which is to say that a very tricky dialect has been rendered with rare simplicity and fidelity into symbols.[42]

Even today, the testimonial aspect of Hurston's work goes ignored in favor of scholarly analyses of Hurston's romanticization of the folk or her often-discussed celebration of African American culture. The blind eye cast to the other issues she addresses draws attention away from the problematic content in Hurston's work, specifically the repeated discussions and depictions of violence against women. Tate reveals an excellent parallel in her discussion of Richard Wright. She aptly notes that in the case of "black canonical novels, like Wright's *Native Son,* the scholarship seems preoccupied with identifying expressions of racial strife, so much so that it effaces other personal conflicts" (182). Critical discussions of Bigger's two murders link them to Wright's social outrage and fail to probe the misogynistic basis of Wright's protest stories, or the "relationship between [his] plots of racial outrage and his repeated use of narrative fragments about female entrapment or betrayal."[43] Likewise, by ignoring the rampant violence that defines the central relationships in Hurston's work, critical discussions of *Jonah's Gourd Vine, Their Eyes Were Watching God,* and *Dust Tracks on a Road* fail to address the violent force that underscores her work.

Critics have also neglected the relationship between Hurston's woman-centeredness and the recurrence of domestic violence within her work. In *Jonah's Gourd Vine, Their Eyes Were Watching God, and Dust Tracks on a Road,* the economic and racially charged settings, set within a system of patriarchy, serve as sites of trauma where various forms of dehumanization occur. These conditions frame what has been described as a "tension" in Hurston's work. Hazel Carby refers to it as a "tension between [her] intellectual consciousness and the consciousness of the folk. . . . [She] brings into being a folk consciousness that is actually in a contradictory relation to her sense of herself as an intellectual."[44] While I agree with Carby that there is a tension between these two forms of consciousness, they are in no way contradictory to Hurston's sense of herself. I would argue that for Hurston, the relation between the folk and the intellectual is a working relationship with a very specific goal of testimony.

This very same working relationship appears in other studies of trauma testimony as well. After an extensive study of the structure of Holocaust testimonies, Saul Friedländer notes the presence of commentary within the testimony. Friedländer finds that "[w]hether . . . commentary is built into the narrative structure of a history or developed as a separate, superimposed text is a matter of choice, but the voice of the commentator must be clearly heard. Such commentary should disrupt the linear facile progression of the narration, introduce alternative interpretations, question any partial conclusion, [and] withstand the need for closure."[45] In other words, the presence of both the narrator and the commentator, or to use Carby's terms, the folk consciousness and the intellectual consciousness, is a common feature of trauma testimony. The function of the intellectual commentator, as noted by Freidländer, is to "disrupt," "question," and "withstand" linear explanations of traumatic—psychically inexplicable—events. Therefore, in the act of trauma testimony, it is the intellectual consciousness that bears the social component and carries the ethical burden of conveying "truth," and it is the folk consciousness that is burdened by the imperative to testify. I suggest that in literary forms of testimony, the intellectual and the folk consciousness work together in an attempt to produce an accurate and ethical narrative through repetition and revision.

Out of this very process of repetition and revision incidents of violence resound in Hurston's work. While she alludes to the impact of economic, racial, and gender bias upon acts of violence, it is important to recognize the simultaneity of these forces and comprehend their presence in her work as fictional attempts to discuss the complexity of experience that is absent in many representations of African American life during her era. The multiple understandings that are particular to imaginative literature become spaces for testimony where the survivor's otherness is naturalized. Hurston's work contributes to the ongoing study of trauma testimony by sifting through the layers of causality and by formulating a culturally specific approach to reading testimony. Also, Hurston's texts map out the negotiations that exist between survivors and secondary witnesses. In order to read her work as testimony, I call upon her historical and regional context, her publishing experiences, personal letters, public reviews, the trauma of her own life, and the trauma that she inherits by virtue of being an African American woman who cannot avoid that "someone [who] is always at [her] elbow reminding [her] that [she] is the granddaughter of slaves."[46]

A large body of Hurston criticism engages in a debate concerning her authority to critique social dynamics outside of her own Eatonville experience. I will argue that it is precisely her personal relationship to the issues she addresses that allows her to create a fiction that calls upon us to see ourselves as accomplices within a tradition of violence against women, violence that is not only a part of the Eatonville tradition but deeply rooted in the western tradition.

Because this project focuses on the impact of domestic violence and gender oppression on Hurston's life and works, I have not offered a substantial discussion of her role in the Harlem Renaissance movement. Suffice it to say that she was a prominent figure in the "esthetics of the Harlem Renaissance . . . help[ing] to lead the revolt of the young artists against 'propaganda' by interesting them in 'pure art' created by the black rural masses" and socially an "extraordinarily witty woman . . . acquir[ing] an instant reputation in New York for her high spirits and side-splitting tales of Eatonville life."[47] The works that I discuss were published in 1934, 1937, and 1942, respectively. Because her childhood and life in Eatonville inform my readings, my central focus is on those periods of her life.

Chapter 1 examines the autobiographical aspects of *Jonah's Gourd Vine* (1934) as a way of locating the source of intergenerational trauma in Hurston's family. By examining Hurston's characterization of her father, John Hurston, I discuss those traumatic events that shaped John's identity and his ability to be a father and husband. In chapter 2, I pay particular attention to the effects that John's legacy of intergenerational trauma has on his relationships with women, especially Hurston's mother, Lucy. Lucy Hurston's deathbed testimony to her daughter and the conditions of her life reveal a great deal about the fictional representation of Zora Neale Hurston, Janie, which appears in *Their Eyes Were Watching God* (1937). Chapter 3 examines the placement and timing of Janie's moments of speech. While engaging the criticisms of François Lionnet, Robert Stepto, Mary Helen Washington, and Hazel Carby, I connect Janie's silence to the temporality that occurs during a period of psychic rupture and interpret her subsequent speech as trauma testimony. Chapter 4 examines Hurston's autobiography, *Dust Tracks on a Road* (1942) as an attempt to master the traumas of her life. Chapter 5 concludes the project with a brief discussion of my own critical interest in the testimonial aspect of Hurston's work and the implications of reading other texts within the African American literary canon as cultural and individual trauma testimony.

CHAPTER ONE

Intergenerational Trauma
in *Jonah's Gourd Vine*

'things dat happened long time uhgo used to seem way off, but now it all seems lak it wuz yistiddy.
You think it's dead but de past ain't stopped breathin' yet.'
—Zora Neale Hurston, *Jonah's Gourd Vine*

In *Beyond the Pleasure Principle,* Freud identifies trauma as the result of "a psychically unprepared encounter with danger."[1] Psychic preparedness can only come when the victim has foreknowledge that he or she will be able to survive the attack. In cases of repeated physical violence and dehumanization, which serves to sustain the victim's vulnerability, the psyche remains "unprepared." Because of this extended state of psychic unpreparedness, domestic violence survivors often feel a persistent vulnerability to violence even after they are beyond the perpetrator's reach. One of the earliest and most brutally honest illustrations of domestic violence as a vehicle for trauma appear in Zora Neale Hurston's first novel, *Jonah's Gourd Vine.*

After four months of intense writing and personal sacrifice, Zora Neale Hurston finished her manuscript of *Jonah's Gourd Vine.* The novel went into publication in May 1934.[2] The largely favorable reviews were due, in part, to critical admiration of Hurston's use of folklore and dialect. Most reviewers found satisfaction in what John Chamberlain describes as a "deep racial rhythm" in the novel.[3] Generally, critics ignored the individual characterizations and the familial relationships in the novel, failing to address even the most troubling aspects of these relationships. The first pages of *Jonah's Gourd Vine* illustrate how the psychological response to repeated violence deeply impacts familial relations in the Crittenden household. During the opening conversation between Ned and Amy

Crittenden, Ned determines that Amy "'needs uh good head stompin'" (1). Surprisingly, the October 1934 issue of the *Times Literary Supplement* describes the novel as "well written and free of the violence often found in novels by Negroes." This blindness to the rampant violence in the novel is directly related to the popular belief that "'Negroes had retained a direct virility that whites had lost through being overeducated.'"[4] As a result, white literary reviewers of the era did not view Ned's beating of Amy as actual violence. It is likely that in this social climate, literary reviewers understood the violence in the novel as a representation of primal expression.

Virility and primal expression notwithstanding, the actual basis for the novel is the lives of Hurston's parents. Robert Hemenway's extensive research of her life and works has led him to the conclusion that *Jonah's Gourd Vine* "is an autobiographical novel."[5] Hemenway goes on to explain that the novel "is usually dealt with as a fictionalization of her parents' marriage—complete with her father's philandering and her mother's steady strength, and Zora's reaction to them both."[6] The novel develops around "John's story [as] [h]e rises from a life as an illiterate laborer to become moderator of a Baptist convention in central Florida." Like Hurston's parents, the novel's "main characters are named John and Lucy; their history is the Hurston family history."[7] Hurston's treatment of her parents' lives takes into account the historical context of their experiences. Hurston's parents, like the fictional John and Lucy Pearson, meet and marry in the small, rural Alabama town of Notasulga. Like John Hurston, the character, John Pearson, moves from being an Alabama plantation worker into a ministerial position in an all-black Florida town. Both John Hurston and his fictional persona are renowned for their powerful poetic preaching; both men are said to have an uncontrollable passion for extramarital affairs, and both marry younger women after their wives die. Also, in both accounts John Pearson and John Hurston are responsible for the family's disintegration after the death of their respective wives.[8] The deathbed scene of Lucy Pearson replicates the actual death of Hurston's mother, Lucy Hurston.[9] Finally, Hurston fictionalizes the tension between John and Lucy Hurston through her depiction of John Pearson's frustration over his inability to psychologically dominate his wife; Hurston "speculated that her father was frustrated by his inability to 'whip [Lucy] mentally.'"[10] Because of its biographical basis, the novel provides valuable insight into Hurston's family history as well as the historical conditions of African Americans during this era.

Through John's development, Hurston underscores the relationship between slavery and gender constructions, class ideals, and race relations among African Americans. For black families during the late nineteenth century, "patriarchal gender relations became crucial signifiers of respectability."[11] During this era, gender roles within the African American community were further complicated by white society's use of sexually charged racial stigmas to deny the morality of black patriarchal gender relations.[12] Using *Jonah's Gourd Vine,* Hurston critiques the late nineteenth-century model of gender relations to reveal the ways that ideologies of race, class, and sexuality support a violent patriarchal social system. By focusing on these issues within her own cultural experience, which includes the history of slavery, I would argue that Hurston locates the violent source of trauma and then attempts to perform a literary act of healing. The ever-present remnants of slavery, in the form of Jim Crow, led her to believe that "the idea of human slavery [was] so deeply ground in that [white Americans] [could not] get it out of their system."[13] Moreover, she was deeply concerned with the ways that slavery and Jim Crow affected the African American community. Using her family's history as the basis for *Jonah's Gourd Vine,* she examines the early years of John's life as an illiterate laborer and historically contextualizes the factors that inspired his initial journey away from home. Unlike the archetypal quest narrative where the hero's call is to adventure, John's departure is a reaction to domestic violence, and the economic and social restraints of his era.[14] Set in 1881 Notasulga, Alabama, Hurston's work addresses the ideological distinctions between antebellum and postbellum African American communities.[15] Ned Crittenden, John's stepfather, reflects his victimization during slavery through what I will call a *postbellum neurosis.*[16] As Hurston demonstrates through the characters of Ned and John, the presence of this neurosis becomes the basis for transmitting intergenerational trauma. One of the many ways that Ned displays this neurosis is by expressing his conviction that "niggers wuz made tuh work" (5). By using the derogatory term "nigger," Ned continues the slaveholder's practice of oppressive and derogatory naming. His belief that African American people, like mules, are on this earth for the single purpose of working demonstrates his neurosis in the form of what Franz Fanon calls an "existential deviation"; this deviation from a humane existence reflects what Ned has learned about his value not as a human being but as property.[17] Ned, after having been the slave of a white man, continues to enslave himself. His ambiguity regarding his identity as a free man combines with his definition of Negro as mule to psychologically maintain his slave status even in a free state. Hurston contrasts Ned's neurosis with Amy's comparatively progressive views. Speaking to Ned, she explains her dreams for her children: "Ah don't want mine tuh come up lak you come nor neither lak me, and Ahm a whole heap younger'n you. You growed up in slavery time"(4–5). While Amy wants her children to have the opportunities of education and free choice, her status as wife and mother limit her ability to act on these goals.

Hurston's fictional ante- and postbellum communities are divided by a creek that John must cross to escape the oppression of his home life. After crossing over, he begins to experience some semblance of independence as he matures into manhood. He marries Lucy Potts, and his never-ending series of adulterous affairs and long absences mark their marriage. Hurston illustrates John's inability to make the transition from plantation-born son of "massa" to independent man as the direct result of his submission to a system of patriarchy that excludes him on the basis of his race but embraces him on the basis of his domination of black women.

The mechanisms of slavery, which she found at work in a variety of forms in both the black and white communities, encouraged Hurston's work. By documenting the historical conditions and memories of her own family experience, Hurston demonstrates the powerful impact of broad sociopolitical practices on a single family unit. She documents the trauma of this relationship by bearing witness to her own familial and cultural experiences. As a result, she should be counted among the early black historians "whose testimonies comprised not only eyewitness accounts of remembered experience but also a set of worldviews with interpretations, analyses, and historical judgments" that are vital to our understanding of her work.[18]

History and Narrative

Hurston's rendering of her own family history through *Jonah's Gourd Vine* includes an economic and historical contextualization of slavery and its powerfully traumatic influence on the shape of her family. Her depiction of Ned Crittenden and the two sides of Notasulga, Alabama, clearly illustrate the postbellum continuation of antebellum relationships informed by cheap labor. Because this discussion ultimately seeks to uncover Hurston's testimony to the effects of trauma, the economics of slavery must be addressed. While I only address these economics in a broad sense, I hope to make clear that "the effective alienation of the black man entails an immediate recognition of social and economic realities. If there is an inferiority complex, it is the outcome of a double process—primarily, economic [and] subsequently, the internalization—or, better, the epidermalization—of this inferiority."[19]

The economics of slavery can be traced to the earliest days of slave importation, which fostered the development of an economic system based on fear and intimidation. It is no secret that the relatively low overhead of slave labor increased agricultural profits.[20] One example that demonstrates the economic benefit of slave labor appears in the parallel between an increased slave population and an increased rate of cotton production; in 1792, America only "produced 6,000 bales [of cotton], [but by 1810] 178,000 bales were produced. . . . Interestingly, [by] 1793, slavery began to flourish in the lower South."[21] Because of slavery's economic advantages, slave owners put forth a great deal of effort to refine the slave system. At various stages in the history of slavery in the United States, slaveholders and the slaveholding states experimented with controlling the number of slaves to maximize the levels of productivity. The aim was to increase levels of production while minimizing costs; fear was the only way to guarantee high levels of production. Slaves "could not be made to work for fear of losing liberty, so they had to be made to fear for their lives."[22]

Slave narratives document the prevalent use of fear as a prime strategy in the effort to control African American slaves. Frederick Douglass reports seeing his master "tie up a lame young woman, and whip her with a heavy cowskin upon her naked shoulders, causing the warm red blood to drip."[23] Many late twentieth-century historians also report the use of violence as the main source of slave control. For example, Edmund S. Morgan finds that slaveowners were often prepared to pay the price of slavery, meaning that "in order to get work out of men and women who had nothing to gain but the absence of pain, you had to be willing to beat, maim, and kill. And society had to be willing to back you even to the point of footing the bill for the property you killed."[24]

By the end of the Civil War, the bill had run very high. The entire nation paid heavily in lost property and lives. Postwar debates were concerned with the actual definition of "free" with regard to freed African Americans. Questions arose as to whether that meant free to vote, free to move anywhere, free to get wages equal to those of whites, and so forth. Whereas white Americans debated the issue, black Americans moved swiftly toward what

> intensive indoctrination had taught them that everyone—white and black—ought to [want]. In the first flush of freedom, black people in the South wanted families; they wanted farms; they wanted schools; and they wanted full citizenship and a recognition of their equal humanity, not only in their governments, but in their churches and in their society.[25]

The freedmen's attempt to claim full citizenship was immediately met with opposition from Southern whites. The level of Southern resistance to the free status of blacks was so intense that by 1866 Congress passed the Freedman's Bureau Bill, giving the military authority to bring to trial and convict persons accused of depriving newly freed African Americans of their civil rights. Resistance to the law continued so that by 1867, Congress passed three Reconstruction Acts that divided the South (except Tennessee) into five military districts. In order to allow black voters access to the polls, these acts established army commanders to control voter eligibility and registration to reduce corruption. Ultimately, these efforts, as well as the passage of the 13th, 14th, and 15th Amendments to the Constitution, failed to provide African Americans with the benefits of full citizenship. The failures of these efforts make clear the impossibility of legislating moral or ethical principles.[26]

Reconstruction came to an end in 1877, as the last federal troops left the South and white Southerners regained control of their state governments. The economy of the former Confederate States continued to be agricultural in nature.

As a result, the desire to continue a cheap labor system of agricultural production did not diminish after Reconstruction. In the absence of military rule, state governments attempted to reestablish many of the practices of slavery.[27] The first generation of free blacks dealt with the determined "effort[s] of Southern whites . . . to restore race relations, in so far as conditions allowed, to some semblance of what they had been . . . in the years before the Civil War."[28] The free status of African Americans altered the ways in which white Southerners went about obtaining the cheap labor they had grown to rely upon. New laws carrying severe penalties suddenly increased the population of black convicts. All across the South, an "almost universal device was to use the courts as a means of reënslaving the blacks."[29] In most Southern states, "convict labor was leased out to private entrepreneurs," creating an opportunity for the middle-man to profit in much the same way the original slavers had.[30] By the mid 1870s, it was clear that

> despite compromise, war, and struggle, the Negro [was] not free. In the backwoods of the Gulf States, for miles and miles, he may not leave the plantation of his birth; in well-nigh the whole rural South the black farmers are peons, bound by law and custom to an economic slavery, from which the only escape is death or the penitentiary.[31]

Those areas of black subjugation that the court system did not enforce were guaranteed by "violence and the great threat of violence . . . [seeking] to lower the self-esteem of blacks and thus render them more controllable."[32] Even today, the full impact of this experience is not completely understood. What is clear is that through music, folklore, dance, parable, religion, and numerous other forms of expression, African Americans continually translate a history of trauma and victimization into a history of survival. While many contemporary critics and practitioners are satisfied with celebrating survival, Hurston's work demonstrates a deeper concern. By focusing on the use of violence within certain African American social contexts, she questions the conditions of survival and their relationship to history.

The Language of Testimony

The factual basis of *Jonah's Gourd Vine* underscores the complex relation between history and memory, particularly the trauma of violent history. The novel shows how the literary, more than any other form of artistic expression, betrays the points of intersection between "language . . . and the psychoanalytic theory of traumatic experience."[33] The language of survivor writing attempts to construct coherent wholes from shattered realities, and as with all narratives, linear stories unfold with a beginning, middle, and an end. However, a central difference between survivor writing and other narrative forms is the noticeable presence of repetition.

When trauma encodes a writer's story, what emerges is a "textual itinerary of insistently recurring words or figures."[34] It is important to note that these recurring figures attain significance above and beyond the traditional literary and theoretical functions; as testimony, the purpose of their literal repetition is to "stubbornly persist in bearing witness to some . . . wound."[35] As readers navigate through this "itinerary," the fictional framework differentiates itself from the trauma testimony. In the literature of Zora Neale Hurston, the recurring figures of silence, departure, and physical acts of violence encode her texts.

Thus, Hurston traces journeys that are compelled by violence and oppressive conditions. Hurston joins a number of writers of her era in calling attention to the ways that violence impacts social relations. One only needs to examine the fiction that emerges in response to World War I and World War II to appreciate the ways in which literature becomes a vital venue for trauma testimony during the twentieth century. A few examples are John Dos Passos *Three Soldiers* (1921), Hemingway's *In Our Time* (1925), Gertrude Stein's *Wars I Have Seen* (1945), and John Hersey's *Hiroshima* (1946). To this we can add the many volumes of testimonial literature and poetry produced by and in honor of Jewish Holocaust survivors. All of these writers "call attention to the ways in which testimony has become a crucial mode of our relation to events of our times—our relation to the traumas of contemporary history."[36]

Like Dos Passos, Hemingway, Stein, and Hersey, Hurston uses a literary format to give cultural and personal testimony to numerous levels of survival. Unlike these writers, however, the external conditions of the trauma she describes are significantly different because they are ever-present. For her contemporaries, trauma describes a rupture, a tear in the perception of themselves and the world once known. Because survivors often fail to consciously register the exact moment of rupture, literature is a prime medium for testimony; "like psychoanalysis, [literature] is interested in the complex relation between knowing and not knowing."[37] This state of not knowing should not be confused with a literal loss of consciousness. Although trauma may induce such a state, its pathologies repetitiously appear in the form of intrusive phenomena.[38] Usually, this temporal state or loss of conscious time is precipitated by an apocalyptic event. This event puts an end to the feeling that there are basic, unchangeable truths about one's existence. In the case of war, many survivors call into question those patterns of behavior that in a prewar state constitute their definition of society and home. For example, in "Soldier's Home" from Ernest Hemingway's *In Our Time* (1925), Krebs, a returning veteran, finds that there are social stipulations attached to his welcome home as the community that he fought for refuses to receive his testimony. He discovers that "to be listened to at all he had to lie, and after he had done this twice he, too, had a reaction against the war and against talking about it" (69). What he receives is time and space to redefine his understanding of his community and adjust to it.

He spends his first months at home "reading a book on the war . . . [and] really learning about the war"(72). This helps to reintegrate him. After reading, he realizes that after all, "[h]e had been a good soldier. That made a difference" (72).

This type of ethical questioning concerning the traumatic event and the need to redefine oneself is consistent with the experience of any *singular* trauma. As Hemingway illustrates through the character of Krebs, survival often leads to an effort to suture one's torn relationship with the world and re-envision an identity that explains one's own survival. This effort is made possible because the traumatic event is singular and because, often, there exists a community of survivors engaged in a similar project.

The clinical definition of posttraumatic stress disorder (PTSD) describes the disruption of an ordered perception of the world. Survivors, having experienced an overwhelming event, were psychically unprepared to attempt to reorganize the experience and *restore order to disorder*. The definition of PTSD assumes the existence of an ordered schema that the survivor understood. The disorder occurs because that schema no longer makes sense. The act of writing is one way that survivors engage in the "art of interpreting" traumatic experience; they can establish a framework for their victimization that simulates preparedness. The term "singular traumatic event" applies to events, like war, that may have lasted for years. The most important of aspect of a singular traumatic event is the presence of a clearly pretraumatized, "normal" ordering of the world that undergoes a rupture, followed by re-entry into normal, pretraumatized conditions.

One of the most distinguishing aspects of Hurston's work is that it gives testimony to a cultural trauma that makes victimization a part of everyday African American experience. The perpetuity of the trauma that Hurston addresses places the victim's experience within the range of ordinary experience. Hurston addresses the personal and cultural trauma that results from living in a *perpetually* violent world while *continually* bearing the "dead-weight of social degradation" and gender discrimination.[39]

In *Jonah's Gourd Vine,* Hurston examines how the violence that is an integral part of American race relations affects numerous levels of social interaction. Because "the family is a miniature of the nation [with] no disproportion between the life of the family and the life of the nation," Hurston's family history is an appropriate model for identifying the violence and resulting trauma of slavery and Jim Crow.[40] Her exploration of her parents' lives within their historical era presents a political and cultural frame for trauma that broadens our understanding of the significant ways our national history shapes communities, families, and individuals.

Because Hurston's work focuses on familial and cultural transmissions, I would argue that she provides one of the earliest and most complex models of intergenerational trauma. Not until recently has intergenerational trauma been understood as reveal[ing] the impact of trauma, its contagion, and repeated pattern within the family. . . . Within an intergenerational context, the trauma and its impact may be passed down as the family legacy even to children born *after* the trauma. . . . Different cultures capitalize on different pathways to acculturate their young. Thus, beyond the familial, from parents to offspring, entire bodies of human endeavor are vehicles of transmission: oral history, literature and drama, history and politics, religious ritual and writing, cultural traditions and the study thereof, such as anthropology.[41]

As a result, the ways in which human groups create "vehicles of transmission" are evident by studying various forms of cultural production in their aesthetics frames.[42] The vast amount of historical scholarship, as well as what is obvious in everyday African American life, makes clear that there are vital cultural mechanisms at work which serve to minimize the effects of hostile race relations in America. Therefore, this study does not, in any way, seek to present a picture of African American culture as crippled by intergenerational trauma. However, inasmuch as we have inherited a legacy of survival, we must acknowledge and seek to understand all aspects of that legacy.

As both trauma survivor and anthropologist, Hurston was in a uniquely discerning position—one that was simultaneously subjective and objective in relation to the events of her era. Her work allows us to examine, through the lens of testimony, culturally specific challenges and responses to the traumas of African American life from the antebellum years to the middle of the twentieth century.

Many of the existing studies of intergenerational trauma focus on the transmission of trauma and its pathologies from a singular event.[43] Using *Jonah's Gourd Vine*, Hurston draws attention to the various forms of enslavement that have been perpetrated upon African Americans in the aftermath of Civil War Reconstruction. As a result, it is difficult to fully align "the notion of a sudden and unpredictable event to an institution that lasted nearly 400 years [.]" Trauma conjures images of victims, pain, and damage; however, slavery was a long-term multidimensional experience involving black victimization as well as effective black coping."[44] Laden with references to these multidimensional experiences, John, the protagonist of *Jonah's Gourd Vine*, emerges as the consummate reflection of his victimization and the patriarchal system that created him. As such, Hurston's novel demonstrates the effects of intergenerational trauma. As the son of a tenant sharecropper, John grows up under the yoke of economic slavery. John is reared on a farm in the rural South, and at the age of sixteen his stepfather, Ned binds him "'over to . . . po' white trash [who] usta' be de overseer on de plantation dat everybody knows wuz de wust in southern Alabama'" (6, 7). The text also demonstrates the extent of economic and psychological control that the ever-present threat of violence exerted on black families in the periods following manumission. Beasley (a white land owner) overcharges Ned for food and supplies. After extracting his payment in cotton, Beasley leaves the Crittendens without enough food to survive. Ned, Amy, and all "'de chillun [had] worked uh whole year. [They] . . . made sixteen bales uh cotton and ain't even got uh cotton seed to show'" (6). Fear of violent retaliation prevents Ned from voicing any objection to the thievery that left his family in poverty. He reminds Amy that "'some of 'em be outside and hear you and turn you over tuh de patter roller, and dey'll take you outa heah and put a hun'ed lashes uh raw hide on yo' back'" (7).[45] This violent threat strips Ned of the ability to provide for his family's needs. It also prevents him from actively protecting his family. His ability to act as husband, father, and head of household diminishes until he can only provide protection in the form of whispered warnings to keep silent about the traumas that organize the decisions of daily existence, including when to look out from your own doorway and what you can and cannot say in the privacy of your home.

Under these traumatic conditions, the call to silence is also a call to co-conspiracy. As Laub suggests, the act of "not telling . . . the [trauma tale] serves as a perpetuation of . . . tyranny. The events become more and more distorted in their silent retention and pervasively invade and contaminate . . . daily life."[46] The presence of this form of tyrannical silencing reflects the social circumstances of African Americans during this time. The contamination of daily life by racist ideology found its way into the subtle behaviors and restrictions that accompanied segregation. These behaviors manifested themselves in a

> process [that] cannot be caught in words that follow one upon the other. White people talking to blacks for instance, was not only a matter of choosing specific words to fall in sequence; it was also a matter of speech inflections, pauses, rises and falls in pitch and volume, of body postures and relative positions, of movements of eyes and hands, of talking down from the porch to the yards.[47]

Each gesture and inflection came with a silent threat. The inherent trauma of this social structure arose because African Americans had little defense. There were few, if any, legal or social mechanisms in place for the protection of African Americans living in the South. At the same time, there was no broad integrated public space to testify to the dehumanizing experiences of the past or present. As a result, the silence around individual and collective trauma perpetuated a psychic tyranny over individual African Americans and their communities.[48] The effects of silencing slavery's 400-year trauma, and its continuation (in an altered form) during Hurston's lifetime, should be explored as a tyranny, which exponentially multiplied its force through the everyday experiences of Jim Crow.

One obvious way that this cultural tyranny surfaces is apparent in the different childrearing practices of white and black America. An old saying states that: "The hand that rocks the cradle rules the world." It refers to the cause and effect relationship between how children are raised to perceive of themselves and the subsequent roles they take on in adult life. Childrearing practices can determine the confidence and success of a child's adult life. These practices are also powerful mechanisms for unconsciously transmitting pathologies of trauma. Hurston voices her concern with how the larger society reinforced low self-esteem and instilled a sense of futility in the minds of black children. In her 1945 *Negro Digest* article "Crazy for this Democracy," Hurston explains: "Jim Crow laws have been put on the books for a purpose and that purpose is psychological. It has two edges to the thing. By physical evidence, back seats in trains, back doors of houses, exclusion from certain places and activities, to promote in the mind of the smallest white child the conviction of First by Birth, eternal and irrevocable. . . . Seeing the daily humiliation of the darker people confirm the child in its superiority, so that it comes to feel it the arrangement by God. By the same means, the smallest dark child is to be convinced of its inferiority."[49] This article chronicles Hurston's continued concern for the psychological impact that the trauma of slavery and segregation had on many African American communities; this concern was initially expressed in *Jonah's Gourd Vine*.[50]

Crossing the Creek

In *Jonah's Gourd Vine*, Hurston presents John's stepfather, Ned, as the character most affected by the trauma of slavery. He is the oldest member of the Crittenden household and grew up as a slave (5). He transmits all of that experience to his children. As the novel opens, John looks out of the door to identify a group of white people passing by, and Ned shouts in fear for him to "'come out dat do' way and shet it tight, fool! Stand dere gazin' dem white folks right in de face! . . . Yo' brazin' ways wid dese white folks is gwinter git you lynched one uh dese days'" (2). Ned's anxiety, manifested in the threat of lynching, effectively keeps the children in a degraded social position. Violent threats simultaneously imprint the child's mind with a historical past, a painful present, and a circumscribed future. Hurston's depiction of the racialized violence and anxiety, which frames the black child's worldview, historicizes the conditions and experiences of untold numbers of African Americans living in postbellum America. Her text serves to "invade hereditary premises and insulations, and [ultimately] open insights to cultural and social forms."[51] As she presents the process of John's maturation, Hurston examines the cultural efforts made to break the cycle of oppression that threatened to bind the next generation.

African Americans used numerous strategies in an attempt to alleviate racial tensions. One way was to raise the self-esteem of children by taking advantage of educational opportunities. The hope was that educating children would transform them, thereby minimizing the negative effects of a traumatic past and present.[52] In *Jonah's Gourd Vine*, Hurston locates educational opportunity on the other side of the creek from where John grows up. John's crossing over to escape Ned and his "slave mentality" symbolically refers to the hope for social mobility that rests in each new generation of African Americans. The setting of John's initial departure from home expresses this hope for new opportunity. At the edge of the Creek separating the two worlds that Hurston juxtaposes, antebellum and postbellum Alabama, she describes a "hunted coon pant[ing] down to the Creek, [swimming] across and proceed[ing] leisurely up the other side," and John, in symbiotic relief, reflecting that with his crossing over, he will experience "no more Ned, no hurry" (12).

John's relief is certainly warranted. Upon reaching the other side, he no longer has Ned to berate or beat him. A new life awaits him. Unfortunately, however, the social circumstances at work in the 1880s in Notasulga, Alabama make a mockery of John's chances for obtaining a full emancipation. Hurston uses the story of this pubescent, first-generation freedman to demonstrate how the economic and social design of the post-Reconstruction rural South was patterned according to the design of the antebellum South. By illustrating this replication of antebellum social structures, Hurston reveals the repetition of an oppressive system which makes John's generation both the inheritors of intergenerational trauma stemming from the legacy of slavery as well as victims of the traumatic, dehumanizing experiences of their own generation.

Those points of social relations between blacks and whites, where change was expected but did not occur, became points of traumatic wounding. Because education was linked to social mobility and inextricably tied to the free status of African Americans, the poor conditions in African American schools broke the promise of opportunity for an entire generation of blacks in the rural South.[53] Many African Americans, like Amy Crittenden, dreamed of their children "gettin' book-learnt" but, as Hurston demonstrates in this novel, the educational opportunities were limited at best (28). For example, the segregated school that John attends is for blacks only and runs for a mere "'three months [before] it's got to close for cotton-picking'" (21). The school's teacher had "little ambition to impart knowledge . . . yearn[ing] [instead] to hold switches in his hand" (25). Within this environment, the children's expectations are extremely low. They are taught to believe that the highest educational goal is to "'spell 'compresstibility,' [since] when you git dat fur 'taint much mo' fuhther fur yuh tuh go'" (27).

For this postwar, postmanumission generation, freedom was threatened every time a social restriction was reestablished. During the post-Reconstruction years, social and political barriers were placed around education, voting, use of public facilities, and economic opportunities. The constant threat to their sense of freedom caused Hurston to note that "when freedom came, it was too much to expect that it would have been acquired immediately."[54] The expectation of an immediate and *actual* transition in status from slave to free was thwarted as much by the external conditions of Jim Crow as by the effects of intergenerational trauma. Through the character of John, Hurston demonstrates how the wounds of Jim Crow worked in conjunction with the historical wounds of slavery to reinforce low self-esteem and a limited vision of personal potential. After crossing over to the "progressive" side of the creek, John's first experience is hearing "a strange noise that [he] had never heard"; it was the noise of "Negro children going to read and write like white folks" (13). However, the effects of having internalized Ned's response to his own trauma immediately overshadows John's excitement: "All this going on over there and younguns over the creek chopping cotton! It must be very nice, but maybe it wasn't for over the creek niggers" (13). By illustrating John's association of his geographical and racial origins with his ability to aggressively pursue an education, Hurston underscores the causal relationship between origins (or history) and education (or potential). She uses this causal relationship to reveal the psychologically crippling effects of traumatic experience. John's initial sense of himself as a misfit in school is one legacy of slavery handed down from Ned, who taught the children that "'all book-learnt niggers do [is]—fill up de jails and chain gangs . . . ; All dese [boys] need tuh learn is how tuh swing uh hoe and turn a furrer. . . . Day ain't goin' tuh no school effen Ah got anythin' tuh say 'bout it. Jes' be turnin' 'em fools!'" (28). The conditions of Ned's upbringing impair not only Ned; when these conditions are handed down, they impair John's ability to see himself as much more than a field hand. Even though he is "amazed at the number of things to be learned," there is little connection between his desire to succeed and a sense of his own intellectual abilities (26, 27). John's primary motivation is sexual. Only after remembering "the black eyes of the little girl in the school yard" does he express a desire for learning: "'Whis ah could go tuh school too'" (19, 26, 27). Once he enters school, his attraction to the smartest girl in school is what drives him to "stud[y] hard because he [catches] Lucy watching him every time he recite[s]" (26). At sixteen years old, John understands his lessons as means to an end and that end is Lucy. He has no concept of education as a powerful force in and of itself nor does he have the full range of educational opportunities available to him. As a result, John's success hinges on his ability to earn a living through hard labor.

During the post-Reconstruction era, the economic opportunities for Southern rural African Americans did not look much brighter than the educational ones. Four years after publishing *Jonah's Gourd Vine,* Hurston prepared a report for the Florida Federal Writers' Project discussing black cultural responses to historical conditions.[55] In this report, called "Art and Such," she describes the post-Reconstruction era as a "matrix," explaining that during this time "what went on inside the Negro . . . has seriously affected . . . every form of Negro expression, including the economic."[56] In *Jonah's Gourd Vine,* she examines the similarities between the economic systems at work in rural areas of the antebellum and post-

Reconstruction South. While living with Amy and Ned, John's limited opportunities to earn a living was manifest in his being bound over to an exoverseer who would pay him poorly in food and maybe provide a suit of clothes for Christmas. This was a common form of reward during slavery. Frederick Douglass reports that slaveholders used the annual distribution of clothing and food rations along with liquor as a means of affirming their paternal positions and "keeping down the spirit of insurrection."[57]

After crossing the creek, however, John's opportunity to earn a living rests with Alf Pearson, the man who had owned his mother and may have fathered him. Alf admits to violently controlling African Americans in his community and on his plantation in his boastful claim that he has "'treed many a coon in [his] time'" (101). As a powerful and wealthy exslaveowner, Alf embodies the system of white paternalism that hinders John's potential for independence. In one of his early conversations with John, Alf explains: "'I'm good to my darkies'" and gives John a new suit of clothes. After all the cotton is picked "and the last load hauled to the gin," Alf reenacts another tradition that was common during slavery by "giving the hands two hogs to barbecue" (28). The black community responds according to the same tradition by making a big celebration and including "Negroes from three other plantations. Some [bring] 'likker'" (28). Whether bound over on Ned's side of the creek to a poor, white exoverseer or working on the "progressive" side for an exslaveholder, John's racial status keeps him economically tied to whites in a system designed to thwart financial independence.

Hurston emphasizes the psychological impact of antebellum practices in the postbellum era by presenting John's easy embrace of the economic system. After arriving at the plantation, John is pleased to learn that Mist' Alf Pearson "ain't gwine overwork [him]. . . . [he will just] hand him his drinks uh drive de carriage fuh him and Ole Miss" (20). John is not at all disturbed by the fact that these are the same "opportunities" that existed during slavery. Instead, he relaxes and "dream[s] new dreams" of an easy life (20). I would argue that John's low expectation of himself as a free man underscores the extent to which he is "convinced of his inferiority."[58]

Because forms of slavery continue on either side of the creek, John remains financially dependent on white men who conceive of him as an inferior, base, and primal being. Cheryl Wall accurately points out that "in [this] period of transition between slavery and freedom, John remains bound by the slaveholder's conception of black men."[59] This is true in regard to almost every facet of John's existence; the ex-slaveholder's conception of his identity dramatically shapes and limits John's life. Nowhere is the impact of his externally defined identity more clearly evident than in John's conception of his sexuality.

By the time Hurston wrote *Jonah's Gourd Vine*, the sexuality of black men as a subject of study had had a few hundred years of notoriety; "the notion that black men were particularly virile, promiscuous, and lusty was [already an old one by] the eighteenth century."[60] The persistent discussion of sexuality and the anxiety over the sexuality of black people in general raise a number of questions about the ways that this particular focus served broad economic and psychosocial needs. Winthrop Jordan explains the psychosocial needs in terms of "white men project[ing] their own desires onto Negroes [since] their own passion for black women was not fully acceptable to society or the self."[61] The obsession with black sexuality is a cornerstone of black-white social relations due to the working relationship between white psychological cleansing and the economic advantage during slavery.

During slavery, a sexually active slave population naturally led to reproduction, which increased the slave stock and the master's economic wealth. In the post-Reconstruction years, the wealth of exslaveholders could no longer be measured in terms of human stock, so the obsession with black sexuality was framed within the discourse of the back beast rapist, which justifies terrorism and segregation. Again, the motivation may be linked to economics. The recession of the 1880s threatened many exslaveholders' ability to provide for their families. As Joel Williamson explains, "there are suggestions that black farmers, so recently out of slavery . . . farmed their lands more intensively than their white contemporaries and that their level of indebtedness tended to be lower."[62] A popular response was to ensure the disfranchisement of black farmers.

One way that whites secured the disfranchisement of African Americans was through the sexual propaganda of the 1880s and 1890s, which promoted the idea that black males were potential rapists to be feared.[63] There was a "particular conjunction of sex and race that seized the South in 1889" and led to the general belief that the South was "virtually besieged by Negro brutes who roamed almost without restraint" desiring to ravish white women.[64] Responding to this myth of black brute sexuality, Hurston places John's maturation within a historically and psychologically deterministic context in order to critique the source of these myths and, more importantly, examine how they affect John's development from boy to man. Her text establishes a "matrix for interrogating how gender and sexuality have been constructed, performed, and policed" by overarching concepts of race.[65]

Black Manhood on the Plantation

John's entrance into the plantation community becomes the setting for his sexual development and his consummate acceptance of a patriarchal definition of manhood. By using the plantation as the setting to explore John's developing sexuality, Hurston places his self-defining and economic impotence on the very same site that applauds his virility. Hurston's text reveals what Hazel Carby so aptly describes as "the relation between political terrorism, economic oppression, and conventional codes of sexuality and morality."[66] The patriarchal manipulation of race and gender ideologies is evident during Alf's first encounter with John. Before acknowledging John's request for work, Alf "stares at him fixedly" and then proclaims him a "stud" who would have "brought five thousand dollars on the block in slavery time" (17).

In this initial meeting between Alf and John, Alf answers John's request for work with a reference to sexuality that is directly tied to his value as a human being. He symbolically affirms his view of John by assigning him to "watch all of [the] brood sows" (20, 21). John does a fine job and eventually earns a promotion, but his access to a "better life" is only available to him because of his alliance with Alf. This alliance is contingent upon his ability to accept Alf's perception of him as a "walking orgasm" (50). By accepting this sexually defined identity, John participates in what Carby defines as the "dialectal relation between economic/political power and economic/sexual power in the battle for control of women's bodies."[67]

By contextualizing John's identity in terms of his sexuality, Hurston rejects the idea that his geographical movement from one place to another, from one side of the creek to another, offers him any real opportunity to develop from a sixteen-year-old boy into an independent man. In the patriarchal sphere of masculine authority, boys become men not by developing sexuality but by developing the skills to provide protection as well as economic and moral support for their families.[68] Mastering the ability to negotiate social and economic circumstances enables men to "fulfill the culturally prescribed roles of provider and protector . . . the key function[s] that our culture identifies with masculinity."[69] Masculine ideals are modeled and transmitted from one male to another. Boys learn how to be men from their fathers and other male authority figures in their lives.[70]

In John's case, Ned's and Alf's definitions of masculinity heavily influence his conception of manhood because they comprise John's most intimate male relationships. For Ned and Alf, John's very existence is understood solely as a result of violence and sexual transgression. While Ned claims to reject John on the basis of the feeble myth that "half-white niggers got de worst part uh bofe de white and de black folks," his rejection has more to do with his perception of John as a living reminder of black men's inability to protect black women during slavery (9). According to the chronology that Amy provides in the narrative, she had to have been only twelve when John was born, and he was born on Alf's plantation. Ned's rejection of John exemplifies how the "maltreatment of women is often considered an affront to the men with whom they are associated. If the slave woman could only escape by 'flight or death,' then the aberration of a system that prevents the stronger members of a group from fulfilling their responsibilities to their dependents is clearly shown. The psychological dejection of those men who could not protect their women is then included as another burden of slavery."[71]

Ned's violent response to John is more of a response to what John represents historically than to John as an individual. Ned tries to meet the emotional obligations that come with being a husband, a father, and head of his household. Unfortunately, John's very existence serves to constantly remind Ned of his slave history and his impotence to protect slave women from rape. As a result, Ned's discussion of John's biracial status prefigures every instance of verbal abuse and physical violence. His inability to accept John as anything more than a "punkin-colored bastard" leads him at one point to try "tuh beat [John] nearly tuh death" (46). Amy's efforts to protect and defend her son incite Ned to "[uncoil] the whip and standing tiptoe to give himself more force, [bring] the whip down across Amy's back" (8). Through his departure, John attempts to escape the racially and sexually charged violence of his home. When John crosses the creek, the only other male model he has to look toward is Alf Pearson.

In Alf Pearson's eyes, John symbolizes the sexual prowess he desires, and at the same time, he is a manifestation of the sexual power he wielded over black women during slavery. His relationship with John's mother remains ambiguous, but the text gives several indications that Alf may have fathered John. First, Amy tells John to go directly to the Pearson plantation and tell Alf that he is her son. When Alf sees John, he notes that John's "face looks sort of familiar, but [he] can't place [him]" (17). He then gives John a suit of his son's clothes and eventually puts John in charge of running areas of the plantation that Alf expected his son to run. Also, Alf gives John the last name of Pearson because he has none of his own. With these inferences, Hurston invites readers to conclude that Alf is John's biological father.

If we are to understand Alf as John's father, then John is proof of Alf's lack of restraint and his participation in the abuse of slave women. He would have had to have raped or, in some other way, coerced Amy, since she was only twelve when John was born. When he refers to John as a "splendid specimen," "a walking orgasm, a living exultation," he affirms his own masculine ideal without ever claiming any responsibility for his actions (18, 50). By telling John that "God Himself was looking off when [he] went and got [him]self born," Alf absolves himself of all crimes against Amy and of all responsibility to John (99). This statement makes John his own father; he "went and got himself born." At the same time, it expresses Alf's hope that God was looking away because John was conceived through the exploitation of an unprotected twelve-year-old, whom he remembers as being a "well-built-up girl" (21). When Alf laughs "heartily" at John's sexual exploits, it is because, in his mind, John manifests both the potential and the result of his own sexual power (50).

Both Alf and Ned engage in transmitting and perpetuating trauma that is organized around patriarchal ideals of kinship between men and domination of women. Because Hurston bases the novel on her own family history, it gives testimony to her father's personal history, his plantation training, and the traumatic legacy of slavery. *Jonah's Gourd Vine* illustrates how these conditions establish loyalties to a violently enforced system of patriarchy. Through the character of John, Hurston examines her parents' relationship and attempts to explain how her father's philandering and violence against women reflect his loyalty to a patriarchal social system that, because of his race, rejects him. This loyalty ultimately robs John of the ability to remain faithful to his wife, his community, and himself. John's adulterous affairs and long absences define his marriage.[72] While Lucy is pregnant with their first child, he maintains sexual relations with a woman named Mehaley, and a sexual relationship with Big 'Oman, followed by sexual relations with Delphine, which was combined with a year-long absence. After moving Lucy and his children to the all-black town of Eatonville, Lucy helps to establish John as town minister. Soon after, people began talking to Lucy about "Hattie Tyson, Oviedo and shame, Gussie, Tillie, [and] Della" (119). John's inability to control his sexual desires affirms Alf's perception of him as "a walking orgasm" (50). Because John accepts sexuality as his defining characteristic, the circumstances of his life are spasmodic and out of control. John expends all of his energies spiraling through failed attempts to fend off what he calls "the brute beast" in him (88).

In addition to John's lack of sexual control, which underscores his failure to be a faithful husband and father, he slaps Lucy. This act of violence precipitates her death. Because the act of violence immediately precedes Lucy's death, Hurston suggests that John's slapping Lucy causes her to lose her will to live. Ultimately, Lucy's death releases John: He "was free. He was sad, but underneath his sorrow was an exultation . . . there was no more sin. Just a free man having his will of women" (136). Shortly after Lucy's death, John marries Hattie Tyson. After a few years of violence and misery, this marriage ends in divorce. He then marries a woman named Sally, and on his way home from an adulterous affair, a train hits John's car.[73]

In *Jonah's Gourd Vine,* Hurston uses the train as a recurring symbol of John's sexuality. Initially "terrified by the 'panting monster,' he is simultaneously mesmerized by this threatening machine whose side 'seemed to expand and contract like a fiery-lunged monster.' As a symbol of male sexuality, the train suggests power, dynamism, and mobility."[74] Because it is both a symbol of John's sexuality and his cause of death, the train serves to deliver Hurston's judgment of John's inability to control his sexual life. By having John's life end as the direct result of the uncontrolled power of the "panting monster," Hurston underscores the destructiveness of a black male identity that is centrally defined by sexual prowess.

Jonah's Gourd Vine provides valuable insight into the historical conditions of post-Reconstruction southern rural areas and the traumatizing use of violence to maintain social control. Through John's development, Hurston underscores the relationship between the violence of slavery and gender constructions, class ideals, and race relations. Her focus on the trauma produced by these conditions provides valuable insight into the legacy of intergenerational trauma and its effect on gender relations. The traumatic conditions of these gendered relationships define the origins of Hurston's black feminist ideals. The examination of her father's life, through the persona of John, allows her to consider the ways that his personal and social history impacted her mother and herself. By writing this novel, Hurston initiates the journey that many black women writers have subsequently taken in search of their own self-defining voices.

CHAPTER TWO

Gender Relations and Testimony in
Jonah's Gourd Vine

> As her father pulled her away from her place above [her mother's] head, Isis thought her mother's
> eyes followed her and she strained her ears to catch her words. But none came.
> —Zora Neale Hurston, *Jonah's Gourd Vine*

In her 1976 essay, "Saving the Life That Could Be Your Own," Alice Walker defines the recovery of Hurston's work as an act that binds her own mother, herself, and Zora together. She explains that if Hurston's story had been lost, then "[her] mother's story would have had no historical underpinning, none [she] could trust. . . . Zora had already done a thorough job of preparing the ground over which [she] was moving."[1] Because of Walker's work, Hurston is now considered the foremother of the African American women's literary tradition. Of her seven published books and numerous short stories, her most overtly feminist work, *Their Eyes Were Watching God* (1937), receives the most critical attention. Because the protagonist is male in *Jonah's Gourd Vine* (1934), critics overlook the feminist aspects of this novel. When reading *Jonah's Gourd Vine* and *Their Eyes Were Watching God* sequentially, however, *Jonah's Gourd Vine* unfolds as part of a developing testimony to the status of black women in the rural South between the 1880s and World War I. The novel gives voice to the racial, sexual, and economic circumstances that contributed to the development of a female-centered black women's discourse. *Their Eyes* responds to the testimony of the women in *Jonah's Gourd Vine* in a number of ways that will be discussed later, but it is through the latter that Hurston first traces the violently enforced confinement and powerlessness of the women who lived a generation before her. She demonstrates what Virginia Woolf had expressed five years earlier in *A Room of One's Own:* "A woman's writing thinks back through her mothers."[2] By writing this novel, Hurston, like Walker, recovers what would have been lost of her mother's and grandmother's stories.

Hurston's exploration of male identity construction in *Jonah's Gourd Vine* examines the ways that silencing, the use of physical violence, and the threat of violence circumscribe limited and often dangerous spaces for women. From a feminist perspective, this novel acts as historical testimony to the traumatic conditions that inspired black feminism. During the nineteenth century, the works of Anna Julia Cooper, Ida B. Wells, and Pauline Hopkins provide examples of texts that focus on women's issues. Their works underscore the racial, sexual, and economic forces that kept black women in vulnerable positions. Hurston's work accomplishes a similar task. However, by focusing on the gendered relationships in her own family and her local community, her texts complicate the image of the oppressor as always white and usually male. Her fiction demonstrates that patriarchal domination comes in a variety of colors and, at times, women participate in sustaining the structure of patriarchal relations. This variation appears in Hurston's depiction of John Pearson as a patriarchal husband and father. Through *Jonah's Gourd Vine,* Hurston demonstrates that, even though John is denied broad access to economic and political power, he is granted access to patriarchal power through the sexual and physical domination of black women, and it is through this domination that John defines his masculinity.

As discussed in chapter 1, Hurston's historical and psychological examination of John's masculine identity gives testimony to the unique set of social circumstances that an 1881 Alabama environment offered. Educationally and economically limited by his social circumstances, John is the product of a deterministic world. His development into manhood conforms to the twisted perceptions of Ned and Alf, the two father figures in his life. As a result, John's adult life is organized around the fulfillment of sexual desire and escape from the subsequent consequences.

Because he never experiences a true climax—a life changing epiphany—John is an underdeveloped character whose sexually framed identity serves to emphasize the more complex qualities of the women in the novel. John's inability to develop beyond the limits of his deterministic environment highlights the vision, determination, and steadfast nature of his mother, Amy Crittendon, and his wife, Lucy Pearson, the personas of Hurston's grandmother and mother. Like most of the men in Hurston's work, John is a static character. Life experiences do not change him.[3] Most importantly, the contrast between John and the female characters of Amy and Lucy allows readers to see how women offer alternative ways of surviving traumatic legacies. The gender relationships in *Jonah's Gourd Vine* serve two primary goals. First, Amy's and Lucy's relationships with their husbands show the initial development of Hurston's black feminist ideal. Second, the gendered relationships in the novel give testimony to the use of violence as a powerful means of maintaining dominance over black women in the post-Reconstruction rural South.[4]

Through *Jonah's Gourd Vine*, Hurston offers a clear analysis of the gender relations that support an oppressive masculine ideal. This oppressive ideal shapes the relationship between John and Lucy; her economic, social, and physical stability is subject to John's articulations of his manhood. Because he subscribes to an oppressive construct of male identity, Lucy suffers the damaging effects of a masculinity that requires supreme dominance and authority over all women. Because John can only articulate and measure his manhood by his ability to possess as many women as possible through sex or violence, Lucy often finds herself alone to fend for herself and her seven children.

By writing *Jonah's Gourd Vine*, Hurston creates a literary vehicle which allows her to reclaim what was lost of her own mother's story. The text serves as a historical and psychological site from which her mother can safely speak. Like her own mother, Lucy Hurston, "Lucy [Pearson] dies an early and unhappy death, emotionally abandoned by John. . . . Zora's strong identification with her mother and her lifelong sorrow at her early death partially explain why Lucy is such a compelling presence" in the text.[5] Lucy Pearson's voice is heard as inner dialogue or in conversation with God. The silences and long periods of abandonment where she alone must support her children speak volumes about her existence. In this work that *seems* to be about John, Lucy's story seeps out from narrow spaces in the text. By telling her mother's story through the character of Lucy Pearson, Hurston establishes this narrow space as a viable place to insert a wedge against silence and complicity. Through family and historical testimony, she relieves women of what Shoshana Felman terms as the "burden of silence and its dead weight . . . [allowing access] to feelings of both mourning and hope."[6]

In what can be described as textual call and response, numerous black women writers followed Hurston's call to testimony in the late twentieth century. In the context of black women's writing, "textual call and response" is a unique cultural framing of what Dierdre Lashgari describes in her use of Bakhtin's dialogics: "[A] constructive discourse of conflict, [which] becomes possible when polyvocal discourse interrupts the dominant monologue. The dialogic process is inherently confrontive, exposing discrepancies, contradictions, rifts."[7] Alice Walker's 1967 collection of short stories, *In Love and Trouble*, Toni Morrison's 1970 *The Bluest Eye*, and Ann Allen Shockley's 1974 *Loving Her* are just a few examples of the "feminist exposure of the injustice with which black women are, [at times], treated by their own men."[8] Through the act of writing, these women express an intolerance for "men in their communities [who] attack as 'disloyal to their people' women who point out connections between gender oppression and other forms of oppression."[9] Like Hurston, they give testimony to both the sexual oppression and liberating possibilities that inform black women's lives. By writing within the context of black cultural experience, black women writers address the reasons to celebrate certain cultural practices and to criticize others. Because their texts are matrilineal in nature, their criticisms should be received within the mothering tradition where "'[t]o be critical of one's culture is not to betray that culture; in fact, it is the withholding of criticism that constitutes betrayal, complicity in holding the community back."[10] Their textual production constitutes a union of women who, through the act of "telling," disobey the rules of patriarchal gender conventions in favor of matriarchal gender relationships that demand testimony and healing. Kai Erickson makes some important distinctions that should be kept in mind as we examine these unions. First, we should think of "traumatized communities as something distinct from assemblies of traumatized persons." Second, the central point is not simply that disaster "strengthens bonds linking people together—it does not most of the time—but that shared experience becomes almost like a common culture, a source of kinship."[11] In the production of black women's testimonial literature, the source of kinship is the testimonial process. Ideally, the testimonial process is simultaneously a type of birthing process where the survivor and her community participate in the delivery, receive what is brought forth, and come together to shape the testimony in a way that will strengthen the community.

Hurston's first two novels are testimonial fictions, which loosen the tongues of black women and "nam[e] as oppressors black men as well as white."[12] Consequently, the testimonial aspect of Hurston's fiction acts "outside black history, [and] writ[es] outside the racial fold."[13] She explicitly disrupts the politically motivated, singular image of the black male as protector of black women, an image integral to late nineteenth- and early twentieth-century Black Nationalist thought. According to Kevin Gaines, popular forms of Black Nationalist ideology equated "uplift and power with patriarchal authority and race integrity with manhood."[14] By telling the story of a black man's sexual exploitation of and violence against black women, Hurston's text could be considered an act of treason against uplift ideology and Black Nationalist thought which held that, regardless of what may actually be going on behind closed doors, images of harmonious domesticity should prevail. W.E.B. Du Bois and others promoted the idea that black women should bear the "primary responsibility [for] carrying the burden of the race by becoming good mothers and thereby creating a better home life. When black women uplift themselves, the race will be uplifted."[15]

The objection to "telling" also underscores class differences between race leaders espousing uplift ideology and the people for whom Hurston speaks. Some of those people were, undoubtedly, women from her own rural Florida town. Hurston's fiction contradicts the efforts of many middle-class black women during her era.[16] Whereas Hurston's fictional response to the subjugation of black women is to give these women voices and mobility, one of the main efforts of "the black women's club movement [was] to persuade poor rural black women in the South to embrace the sexual morals of the Victorian middle-class."[17]

During Hurston's lifetime, African American leaders generally felt it was best not to publicly mention the "internal tensions of class, gender, sexuality, and color [because] when one recognized the inconsistencies between black bourgeoisie ideals and conduct, [it was clear that] claims of race solidarity could not withstand the devastating realities of segregation and poverty."[18] Part of these realities include the persistent exploitation of black women by white men; "the continued sexual assault of black women after slavery in both the North and the South prompted black men and women alike to write popular magazine articles appealing to the American public to put a stop to this abuse."[19] During the late nineteenth and early twentieth centuries, black women in the rural South, with limited means of economic support and minimal education, had little opportunity to escape the abuse of the men they were dependent upon.

As a product of this era, Hurston was greatly affected by her status as a relatively poor, black female born in the rural South. By giving voice to her mother's and grandmother's experiences, she forges an ethical relationship between her historical identity and the experiences of her everyday life. These everyday experiences include Hurston's own personal dealings with Jim Crow and economic oppression, which caused her to work on and off as a domestic from the time she was fourteen years old until she was 59. Cheryl Wall's fine chronology of Hurston's life cites the following years of domestic service: In 1905 Hurston scrubbed stairs and cleaned the kitchen to pay her school bill. Between 1906 and 1911, after the Hurston children were dispersed among aunts and uncles, she worked on and off as a domestic. From 1915 to 1916, she worked as a maid for the Gilbert and Sullivan troupe. In 1917 and 1918, while waiting to enter Howard University Preparatory School, she worked as a maid to earn room and board, and in 1950, she worked as a maid in Miami.[20] Hurston publicly expressed the outrage she felt when in 1931, three years before publishing *Jonah's Gourd Vine*, a racist New York physician refused to see her in an examination room and placed her instead in a "closet where the soiled towels and uniforms were tossed . . . [her seat] was a chair wedged in between the wall and the pile of soiled linen."[21]

In response to all of these factors, Hurston's fiction deliberately "raise[s] the issue of ethical behavior in the teeth of the survival imperative" that she struggled with in her own lifetime.[22] Her works attempt to ethically negotiate the relationship between her historical identity as the granddaughter and the daughter of brutally silenced women and the traumas of her own life. The result is a refusal to erase her mother's or her grandmother's histories. In fact, by giving them a voice, she rejects, for herself and other black women, an externally imposed historical identity that is framed by a history of violence and oppression.[23] Instead, she chronicles women's transformational power over trauma.

Transforming Trauma

The power to transform a traumatic experience should not be understood as a psychic erasure of the event. Threatening social events trigger the force of traumatic histories and become a source of controlling marginalized groups who are "aware of the potential for repeated victimization."[24] In *Jonah's Gourd Vine,* Hurston contrasts Ned's participation in the transmission of intergenerational trauma with Amy's desire to encourage her children to live as free men. By insisting that his children be raised like him, as slaves, Ned becomes the vehicle of a traumatic trigger (4). Amy receives the news that Ned has bound John over to a white planter as a trigger that recalls her traumatic experiences during slavery; "in a frenzied silence, [Amy] . . . noticed that the rain had ceased; that the iron kettle was boiling; that a coon dog struck a trail way down the Creek, and was coming nearer, singing his threat and challenge" (7). The threat and challenge of the coon dog aligns John's being bound over for labor to being reduced to the status of a slave. Because dogs were used to hunt down runaway slaves, also known as coons during slavery, Amy's perception of the coons as "coming nearer" measures the extent of her continued vulnerability. Her "frenzied silence" serves to partly define her relationship with "a crisis that is not yet over."[25] However, she defines the other aspects of her relationship to the perpetual crisis of her life when she refuses the mantle of victimization and attempts to protect her children.

Out of the desire to protect her children, Amy preaches that even if it "'take[s] some of us generations us got tuh 'gin tuh practice on treasurin' our younguns'"(5). In spite of Amy's own traumatic origins and the fact that she is, to an extent possessed by the trauma of her life, she is not, like Ned, a dehumanized product of her experiences. Hurston links Amy's ability to transform her own oppressive history into a source of vision and resistance to her role as a mother. When Ned approaches John with a whip, Amy rises

> like a black lioness [and says] "Ned Crittendon, you raise dat wood at mah boy, and you gointer make a mad nigger outa me . . . anytime you tries tuh knock any dese chillun 'bout dey head wid sticks and rocks, Ah'll be right dere tuh back dey fallin'. Ahm dey mama." (2, 3)

By contrasting the characters of Amy and Ned, Hurston establishes a vital link between motherhood and an ethical call to resistance against the transmission of trauma.[26] Amy's willingness to use her own bruised body to cushion her children's fall dramatically underscores Hurston's vision of motherhood as a source of resistance.

As a former slave, Amy shares a distinct and intimate legacy with Ned; at the same time, her individual experiences as a slave were complicated by her gender. Hurston presents the differences between male and female experiences of slavery in terms of her character's inner strengths. For example, even though Amy is beaten and abused, her spirit is not broken. While she was a slave girl, she had no means of self-defense. Now that she is free, she does not cower in fear acting as if she still has no defense. Instead, Amy fights against domination, regardless of whether or not she can win. One scene that demonstrates Amy's fighting spirit describes Ned's actions when he sees no dinner plate prepared for him. He brings "the whip down across Amy's back." Instead of reacting in broken submission often associated with victimization, "the pain and anger kill[s] the cry within her," and using her pain and anger as a revolutionary source of strength she "wheel[s] to fight." Although Ned dominates Amy, his ability to dominate her is always contested. Battling was not new to her; "this had happened many times before" (8). Even though he may win the fight, Amy never makes it easy for him to do so; her "strength was almost as great as Ned's and she had youth and agility with her" (8). She fought Ned at all costs, and when Ned saw that "victory for him was only possible by choking Amy, he thrust his knee into her abdomen and exerted a merciless pressure on her throat" (8). Amy cannot win the physical battle, but by fighting, she wins the ethical battle against easy submission to violent oppression.

The lesson that Amy imparts to other women is to fight back, regardless of whether or not they can win; through the act of fighting, she asserts her own humanity. Amy's decision to stay with Ned in a violent and oppressive relationship also demonstrates how Amy participates in maintaining her own status as a free human being. For example, Amy could take herself and her children across the creek and leave Ned, yet she refuses to go without him. Amy's decision to stay with Ned reflects her decision to claim final authority over the use of her body. She would rather "strain wid Ned" than with the exslave owner who impregnated her at the age of twelve (11). Remembering Amy as "a well-built-up girl and a splendid hoe hand," Alf Pearson is baffled as to why she "married that darky and let him drag her around share-cropping (21). Amy chose to live with "welts on her face and body" on the side of the creek where cotton was the only thing that bloomed rather than submit to Alf (11, 12). Staying with Ned does not prevent Amy from being possessed by a man, but it takes the decision of who that man will be off of the auction block and places it in her own hands. The significance of Amy's ability to choose may appear minimal since she remains subject to male domination. However, the fact that she has any choice at all is crucial to tracing the evolution of Hurston's feminist ideal and its relation to Amy's history as a slave girl.

Claiming Women's Bodies

Under the yoke of slavery, women were vulnerable to sexual exploitation by overseers and masters alike. In *Jonah's Gourd Vine,* Hurston implies a coerced sexual relationship between Alf Pearson and Amy. Amy's subsequent choice to remain married to a man who beats her rather than return to Alf's plantation demonstrates Amy's "struggle for sexual autonomy . . . [and] her determination to control her own body."[27] By refusing her exmaster access to her body and consenting to give Ned access, she exercises relative control over her own sexuality. While she never achieves sexual autonomy in the absolute sense, she exercises the right to choose who will and who will not have access to her body. Amy's choice articulates a "code of ethics emphasiz[ing] a woman's prerogative to . . . govern the integrity of her body."[28] For Hurston's grandmother and other rural black women of her grandmother's era, the struggle for sexual autonomy was an ongoing battle. Amy's hard-won battles with her husband transform the crippling effects of a traumatic history of violence and exploitation into a relative victory of sexual independence. The battle for black women's sexual independence emerges in Hurston's fiction as part of an unfolding testimony to women's need to "be about the task of providing for [their] own spiritual and physical survival because an oppressive male-dominated world conspires to make [them] beast[s] of burden."[29]

Interestingly, Hurston presents the agents of sexual oppression and liberation as both male and female. She avoids monolithic representations of African American men and women by including depictions of fathers who support their daughters' right to choose sexual mates and mothers who support the patriarchal domination of their daughters. Lucy's father, for example, stands against his wife's objections to John as a suitable husband, and after telling his wife to "'dry up! [since Lucy] done done her pickin,'" he "tucked Lucy into the buckboard and drove the silent little bundle to the church huddled against him. His arm about her gave his blessing" (78, 79). Lucy's mother works toward keeping patriarchal gender relations in place. For economic reasons, Lucy's mother, Emmeline Potts, arranges a marriage for Lucy: "Artie Mimms is wid sixty acres under plow and two mules and done ast me fuh yuh ever since yuh wuz ten years old and Ah done tole 'im he could have yuh'" (77). Because Emmeline is concerned that Lucy have a "[a man] dat kin feed [her]" she, in effect, places Lucy on an auction block to the highest bidder when she is only ten years old (77). Emmeline's actions establish her complicity within the very system of patriarchy that Amy and Lucy resist by choosing their own mates. The fact that, like Amy, Emmeline is a mother, demonstrates the various ways in which individuals respond to traumatic social conditions. Some, like Amy, come out fighting to the death, and others, like Emmeline, seek safer spaces of survival. Emmeline's motherly response is to keep her daughter "safely" within the system of patriarchy where money and marriage offers some semblance of protection. In contrast, Amy's motherly response reflects the desire to transmit to her children a fighting spirit, which rejects domination. While Amy and Emmeline represent two different responses to their gendered social positions, young Lucy reflects a new generation of women. As such, Lucy becomes the point of access to her own daughter's history and a source for decoding social systems that try to use her as a vehicle of domination.

Rejecting Emmeline's command that she marry for sixty acres, Lucy enters her marriage by initially transgressing the existing boundaries of patriarchy. As a progressive young woman of her generation, Lucy negotiates the expected role of female submission to authority with her own perception of womanhood. The distinction between Lucy and her mother and mother-in-law illustrates the evolution of black women's feminist ideology over time. Lucy's mother-in-law, Amy, understands her progress as a woman in terms of her ability to remove herself from Alf Pearson's sexual exploitation. Lucy's mother, Emmeline, understands progress in terms of the ability to place her daughter under the protection of an economically stable male. Lucy understands women's progress in terms of severing the relationship between economics and marriage; she marries for love. Lucy's willingness to defy her mother and fight for her right to choose a sexual partner is evident when Emmeline threatens to beat Lucy for marrying John. Lucy asserts ownership of her own body and proclaims that she "'ain't takin' no whippin' tuhnight. All mah switches done growed trees'" (78). Lucy's heroic effort to define herself as a woman with the right to choose to whom she will give her body is a pivotal gesture in the formation of her own autonomy.

Even though the distinction between Lucy and her mother marks the ideological difference between two generations of black women, the circumscribed boundaries of African American life in the 1880s meant that Lucy, like those before her, remained subject to male domination.[30] Lucy's relationship with John reveals how his notion of manhood serves to oppress her; it also demonstrates how she uses her position as a mother to transmit a sense of autonomy to the next generation of women. Hurston presents Lucy's desire to bequeath an ideology of independence to her daughter as the direct result of the domination present in her marriage to John.

Lucy's position as John's wife demands that she immediately relinquish her newfound sense of independence and womanhood. On their first night of marriage, John establishes the limits of Lucy's autonomy. He invites her total dependence by promising "'tuh be a father and mother tuh [her]'" (79). John's masculine fantasy does not allow consideration of an equal partnership with Lucy. Instead, he measures his level of manly strength against what he conceives of as her weaknesses. Hurston underscores the paternal nature of his promise by having John refer to Lucy as a "'girl chile.'" As such, he asks that she "'jes' look tuh [him]. Jes' put [her] 'pendence in [him]. [He] means tuh prop [her] up on eve'y leanin' side'" (79).[31]

The cruelty of John's attempt to make Lucy entirely dependent on him emerges in his absolute failure to consistently provide support for her or their children. Constantly led by sexual desire, John is often absent when his family is in need. For example, in the ninth month of Lucy's fourth pregnancy, John begins a new affair that keeps him "away from home . . . almost continually" (89). Lucy is left alone, pregnant, with no money and little food. She finds herself having to fend off debtors. The fact that one debt is owed to her brother, Bud, makes little difference in the way he treats her. Outraged that Lucy refused to marry Mimms and the sixty acres, her brother taunts her by telling her that John is "'layin' all 'round de jook behind de cotton gin wid Delphine'" while she is "'cooped up wid three l'il' chillun in uh place ain't big uhnough tuh cuss uh cat in'" (91). Condemning Lucy for daring to choose her own marriage partner, Bud points out that "'if [she] wuz married tuh anybody [she] wouldn't be in no such uh fix'" (91). In lieu of the three dollars that Lucy owes him, Bud moves Lucy out of the way, tears down her wedding bed, and takes it with him. Pregnant and abandoned by her husband, punished by her brother for not acquiescing to patriarchal mandates that call upon her to sell herself to the sixty acres and two mules that Artie Mimms represents, Lucy is left "crumpled in a little dark ball in the center of the [mattress]" with her five-year-old son crying "'Mama, Ah Hungry'"(91). Before the night ends, Lucy gives birth with the help of the three elder women in the plantation community. Alone, without the husband who promised to prop her up on every leaning side, Lucy's sole support comes from the women of her community who comfort her and provide food for her and her children (79).

Because he is primarily a sexually defined man, John fails to consistently act as a husband and provider for Lucy and their children. After returning home from his mistress, he uses violence and thievery to try to repair the damage of his neglect. He begins by taking revenge on Bud and beating him. To feed his family he steals a pig and slaughters it. In his conversation with Lucy, John attempts to hide his failure and make Lucy a party to the cover-up. He asks her to affirm his role as provider by reminding her that she "'got uh *man* tuh fend fuh [her]'" (95). As a result of John's thievery and violence, he faces the prospect of the chain gang. To avoid prosecution, he accepts Alf's help and, for a year, leaves Lucy and four children with no visible means of support. By presenting Lucy as a victim of a male "standard that frees men and bridles women," Hurston emphasizes the traumatic consequences of gender oppression.[32]

Violent Control, Coercive Unions

In addition to the economics that bound women during Lucy's era, *Jonah's Gourd Vine* interrogates the patriarchal social system that condones the use of violence as a way of maintaining control over women. In the case of Lucy and John, violent actions and the threats he makes against her underscore his desire to strip her of all agency and leave her in childlike dependence on him. John's method of controlling

Lucy follows the classic pattern of violence and dominant behavior that Laura E. Tanner explores in *Intimate Violence: Reading Rape and Torture in Twentieth-Century Fiction*. As Tanner explains, the dynamics

> of violence often involve a violator who appropriates the victim's subjectivity as an extension of his own power. . . . Acts of intimate violence, then, transform human interaction into a struggle for power in which the victim is stripped of the ability to define and control his or her participation [in the relationship].[33]

John's most aggressive act of maintaining power over Lucy follows a conversation where Lucy tells him that if he wants to leave, there are other men interested in her. John's response is to swear that if she says that again he is "'goin' tuh kill [her]'" (110).[34] The sexual nature of his propriety over her is violently reinforced in the setting of this scene, where he sits on the edge of the bed with a loaded Winchester and declares that he's "'de first [man] wid [her], and [he] means tuh be de last. Ain't never no man tuh breathe in [her] face but [him]'" (110). To ensure that Lucy understands the limits of her autonomy, John explains: "'If you ever start out de door tuh leave me, you'll never make it tuh de gate. I means tuh blow yo' heart out and hang fuh it'" (111). Shortly after John makes this statement, with the loaded Winchester still within his reach, Lucy proclaims her undying love for him. Because this coercive scene is set on the edge of their marriage bed, it opens up a "forum for considering the overriding connections between a woman's body as a site of violence and violation and as a source of life."[35] The incongruity between the threat of violence and Lucy's immediate declaration of love disrupts the narrative of romantic love by creating an ideological gap between marital love as a source of life and the death threat that binds Lucy to John.

The violent source of this incongruity establishes one of the testimonial aspects of the novel. As previously discussed, *Jonah's Gourd Vine* is based on Hurston's family history. In Hurston's 1942 autobiography, *Dust Tracks on a Road*, she discusses the origins of this scene and the novel's general representation of her parents' marriage. In *Dust Tracks*, Hurston says that she knows her

> mother was very unhappy at times, but neither of them made any move to call the thing off. In fact, on two occasions I heard my father threaten to kill my mother if she ever started toward the gate to leave him. . . . on another occasion. . . . Papa marched her into the house with the muzzle of his Winchester rifle in her back. . . . I take it that Papa and Mama, in spite of his meanderings, were really in love. (10, 11)

In both texts, Hurston testifies to intimate love relations that are set within a violent context. Through her initial telling in *Jonah's Gourd Vine,* and her retelling in *Dust Tracks on a Road,* she forces readers to question the basis and validity of a love that is violently enforced. By questioning the foundation of this relationship, Hurston aggressively uses her narratives to establish herself as a "storyteller with a mission; [her] responsibility as survivor is to bear the tale" of her grandmother's and her mother's lives.[36] By doing so, she undoes the myth of domestic bliss and questions the entire basis of violently enforced male-female relationships.

Throughout the course of *Jonah's Gourd Vine,* Hurston presents Lucy's position as potentially powerful but ultimately oppressed. Lucy teaches John all he needs to know to be a leader in the community; "John had to be pushed and shoved and there was no one to do it but Lucy" (116). His success is predicated on her advice, and Lucy's vision ultimately gives shape to John's vague and transient existence. Her role in his success is evident shortly after John is called to preach. Lucy teaches John that if he "'jus' handle[s] [his] members right . . . [he's] goin' tuh be a sho 'nuff big nigger'" (112). Lucy takes control of guaranteeing John's success in the community. She explains to John, "'you lissen tuh me. Ah hauled de mud tuh make ole Cuffy. Ah know whuts in 'im'" (112).[37] Lucy's sound advice on the ways of men is given and received solely on her authority as a woman and mother. However, she is bound to John, regardless of his actions against her, by economics and violent threats. Ironically, because Lucy's authority as a woman and mother stems from externally defined gender constructions, it is appropriated by John and used as the basis of domination.[38] John succumbs to Lucy when she offers economically or socially advantageous advice. When Lucy's advice does not benefit him, he silences her with threats of violence. In this narrative, Hurston links violence against Lucy to "the beginning of the end for John; his public fortunes decline, and his private life falls into disarray" after he slaps Lucy.[39]

After Lucy's death, John spends his remaining years in violent and oppressive relationships with women.[40] First, he marries Hattie Tyson. Guilt-ridden by his violent act against Lucy, John "beat [Hattie] severely and felt better. Felt almost as if he had not known her when Lucy was sick. He panged a little less. So, after that he beat her whenever she vexed him. More interest paid on the debt of Lucy's slap" (145). After divorcing Hattie, John leaves town and marries Sally, a woman who is financially independent and generous with John. The first time John leaves home for a few days, he betrays Sally with a young girl by the name of Ora. Angry with Ora and blaming her for his own sexual weakness, John "viciously thrust her away from the car door without uttering a word. He shoved her so hard that she stumbled into [an] irrigation ditch" (199). Hurston ends the novel shortly after this scene, with John's car being struck by a train.[41] As mentioned in chapter 1, because it is both a symbol of John's sexuality and his cause of death, the train serves to deliver Hurston's judgment of John's inability to control his sexual life.

In contrast to John, Lucy learns from the hard lessons that life teaches her. Looking back on her life, Lucy finds that she has spent it "'in sorrow's kitchen and [she] done licked out all de pots . . . done died in grief and been buried in de bitter waters, and . . . done rose agin from de dead lak Lazarus. Nothin' kin touch [her] soul no mo'" (131). While she realizes that it is too late to benefit from her own hard-won wisdom, she knows that it is not too late for her daughter, Isis. At the very moment when Lucy appears to have been slapped into an early grave, she claims control of her life by defining its significance. She attempts to transform the traumatic legacy that her daughter will inherit as a result of being reared in a home where the primary relationship was violently enforced. Lucy transforms this legacy by engaging in a motherly tradition of orally passing on to her daughter all that she has learned from her experiences.[42] The act of passing on all of the wisdom and advice to her daughter recasts her role as mother. Lucy is no longer a mother solely because she bore seven children but also because she bequeaths mechanisms of survival to her daughter.

By giving testimony to her life "in sorrow's kitchen," Lucy reconfigures herself. She becomes a powerful mother whose words, ultimately, have the authority to psychologically unbind other women. The imperative behind her testimony attacks the pernicious systems of sexism, racism, and poverty. Through her act of testimonial transmission she builds a bridge between two generations of women, her own generation and her daughter's. Lucy's deathbed testimony destroys the existing notion of powerless females by bequeathing to her daughter a vision of self-preservation and autonomy. Lucy warns her daughter to guard against loving anyone "'better'n you do yo'self. Do, you'll be dying befo' yo' time is out. . . . uh person can be killed 'thout being struck uh blow'" (130). She leaves a blueprint for living with her daughter that includes a vision of economic independence. She urges Isis to "'git all de education you kin. Dat's de onliest way you kin keep out from under people's feet'" (130).[43]

The Call to Bear Witness

Lucy's last words serve as a testimony and as a guide for other women. She speaks from the authority of her experience within a social system that placed women in a subjugated position. As Hurston makes evident through Lucy's life, often when violence enforces subjugation, victims perceive the "trauma [as] a natural extension of their powerlessness."[44] However, women such as Hurston's mother and grandmother seem to understand the traumatic conditions of their lives as an extension of their powerlessness without viewing these conditions as natural. By using her last energies to transmit an alternate ideal to her daughter, Hurston's fictional mother, Lucy, ends her life with a call to battle to which her daughter must respond. She effectively casts Isis in the role of a witness who bears a responsibility to define and articulate the meaning of life for herself and other women. The potency of Lucy's call to battle lies in its ability to render patriarchal domination impotent by instigating the formation of women's communities engaged in a variety of testimonial projects.

Because *Jonah's Gourd Vine* depicts the victimization of women in Hurston's family, it can be understood as a prelude to her exploration of the transforming potential that exists in the testimony of surviving women. Through *Jonah's Gourd Vine,* Hurston begins to "acknowledge the tangible and confusing effects of ideology and history . . . [and she] examines the possibilities for grace in the aftermath of brutal oppression"; this possibility engenders a reclamation of violent historical and personal pasts while envisioning a future [that] explor[es] a balance between the claims of history and the need for moving forward.[45] The testimonial aspect of Hurston's works calls upon women to move forward, but not in social patterns that repeat her own mother's confinement and oppression. Her work exposes the gendered conditions of women in the two previous generations of African American women and demonstrates the need for early twentieth-century women to use the comparable freedoms that modern women are afforded to redefine concepts of womanhood and motherhood. In her second novel, *Their Eyes Were Watching God* (1937), published just three years after *Jonah's Gourd Vine,* Hurston introduces a modern, female heroine who uses the act of giving testimony to transform the notion of mothering by aligning it with narrative production.

CHAPTER THREE

Testimony and Reproduction in
Their Eyes Were Watching God

She had found a jewel down inside herself and she had wanted to walk where people could see her
and gleam it around. But she had been set in the market-place to sell. Been set for still-bait.
—Zora Neale Hurston, *Their Eyes Were Watching God*

In the introduction to his edited collection of essays *Reading Black, Reading Feminist* (1990), Henry Louis Gates argues that the texts of black women engage in conversation with one another. From this ongoing textual conversation between black women writers, a conversation heard in "formal echoes, recast metaphors, even in parody—a 'tradition' emerges and is defined."[1] The black women's literary tradition that Gates refers to is based, in part, on the subject position of black women writers, whose early literary images demonstrate the "appropriation by men of power to define tradition."[2]

As the unrivaled literary foremother of twentieth-century African American women writers, Zora Neale Hurston is an appropriate resource for locating the originating sounds of what Gates refers to as "formal echoes and recast metaphors." What emerges from close readings of Hurston's work is, as Gates claims, the formation of intimate literary relationships through the works of writers such as Alice Walker, Sherley Anne Williams, and Gwendolyn Brooks.[3]

The impetus behind the formation of these intimate literary relationships is discernible only when the textual conversations are examined through the frame of trauma and testimony. Because African American women writers share a unique history and position within American culture, their works should be understood primarily as testimonial in nature. Testimony can be understood as simply telling or testifying to events as they occur. As Gwendolyn Mae Henderson explains, black women are engaged "in a discourse that [is] characterized as primarily testimonial, resulting from a similar discursive and social positionality. It is this commonality of history, culture, and language which, finally, constitutes the basis of a tradition of black women's expressive culture."[4] The shared social position, history, culture, and language that "constitutes the tradition of black women's expressive culture" cannot be fully understood until the *traumatic impact* of these constituting elements are examined and defined. There is an inextricable link between trauma, survival, and the ethical imperative to give testimony. In the tradition of public witnessing, trauma testimony aims to disrupt "not only individual isolation but a wider historical isolation that . . . is communicated on the level of our cultures."[5] For example, introducing her second edition to *Witnessing Slavery*, Frances Smith Foster describes the personal impact of receiving testimony by recalling how "slave narratives ma[d]e [her] a witness to slavery, [and by becoming a witness, the texts] undermined the arguments of those who asserted that their [only] value lay in the accuracy of [their] representation[s]."[6] Slave narratives do not merely provide historians with data concerning the institution of slavery. More importantly, these narratives, establish an American literary tradition propelled by an ethical imperative to give testimony to the psychological and physical trauma of slavery.

The transformational power of trauma testimony exists in its ability to take the experience of psychic rupture and use it to form healing communities. As Tal writes, the most "important factor in women's decisions to testify to atrocity is the feeling of sisterhood, of connection to other women, and the hope that the community of women will be strong enough to prevent the commission of atrocities in the future."[7] When read as testimony, Hurston's works reveal how this particular literary tradition of witnessing functions as a weapon to combat the social systems that would have black women believe their identities are primarily circumscribed by constructions of class, race, and gender. Indeed, an analysis of the intertextuality of black women's works does establish their works as constituting a tradition of conversational literary activity. To view them solely as conversation, however, diminishes the ethical imperatives behind the many volumes of black women's literature that now exist. To understand the *ethical activity* that Hurston's texts promote, her work must be read as *constituting a tradition of testimony*.

The intertextual discourse that Gates correctly understands as *identifying* the social implications of sexuality, race, and class thus means little without the *ethical dimension* that calls for liberating action. Reading Hurston's work as part of an ethical project of testimony demonstrates how the act of literary testimony instigates the practice of publicly identifying human violations and the violators. In fact, in writing testimony, victims practice what Dori Laub calls a "mode of struggle against the victims' entrapment in trauma repetition, against their enslavement to the fate of their victimization."[8] Hurston's testimonial project unmasks the offenders and records the violence inflicted against women into the memories of all who read her works. As a result, she not only establishes an important tradition, but she also radically resituates the roles of sexuality, kinship, race, and class distinctions in African American women's writing.

A Radical Heroine

By reading *Their Eyes Were Watching God* as an ethically driven testimony to personal and historical trauma, we can begin to fully understand the impetus behind Hurston's desire to radically disrupt those social orders that sought to entrap women in a variety of ways. In 1937, Hurston wrote *Their Eyes* in seven weeks while on a Guggenheim fellowship in Haiti to research Obeah practices in the West Indies.[9] The novel presents an unusual figure in American letters—a poor, black, rural, questing woman whom Hurston calls Janie Crawford. While much of the novel is set in a small Florida town that recalls Hurston's own Eatonville, Janie travels, marries, gains wisdom, and returns to pass it on.

Because the novel is told retrospectively, Janie's narrative begins as she returns home. Her actual quest begins as her pubescent sexuality emerges. Janie defines sexual communion through the natural process of reproduction—specifically through the image of a "pear tree soaking in the alto chant of visiting bees" (11). In contrast to this image, Nanny, Janie's grandmother, forces her into a marriage with Logan Killicks, an old man with a home and sixty acres. When the marriage falls short of her vision, Janie runs off with Jody Starks, who brings her to an all-black Florida town (16). As mayor of the town, Jody's words become law while Janie is virtually silenced. After Jody's death, Janie marries a younger man, Tea Cake, and her journey continues as they travel together to the South Florida Everglades, or the "Muck." There, Janie finds her own voice, and he teaches her important lessons about survival, including how to shoot a gun. After accidentally becoming infected with rabies, Tea Cake turns on Janie, and in order to save herself, she shoots him. Their relationship reflects both Janie's joy at having found her pear-tree love and the sorrow of his death. The narration takes place in the intimate setting of Janie's porch. As Janie gives her story over to her "kissin' friend" Pheoby, a transformation occurs that causes Pheoby to "'[grow] ten feet higher from jus' listenin'" (7, 192).

As Pheoby's transformation demonstrates, *Their Eyes* is a compelling tale driven by Hurston's demand for altered conceptions of women's identities. The questing heroine was, during Hurston's lifetime, a radical figure. Not only does Hurston's heroine leave an oppressive yet secure community in search of selfhood, but she honors the ethical demand to give testimony to other women, encouraging them to first define and then satisfy their own passions. *Their Eyes* demonstrates Hurston's personal commitment to this demand, which stems from the fact that the text also seeks to portray her own inner self. As Elizabeth Fox-Genovese notes, *Their Eyes* "offers Hurston's most sustained attempt to provide some representations of her own emotional life."[10] Hurston fashions herself in the character of Janie as a way of giving testimony to the violence and oppression she encountered in intimate relationships between men and women. This novel also adds her testimony to that of other women, particularly her mother and grandmother, whose lives she examines through the characters of Lucy Potts and Amy Crittendon in her first novel, *Jonah's Gourd Vine* (1934).

Janie's ability to exude independence and wisdom depends on an understanding of the women in *Jonah's Gourd Vine,* which situates Hurston's perspective on womanhood relative to her own family history. Her capacity for independence and wisdom are legacies from Amy Crittenden, Lucy Potts, and the other women of Notasulga, Alabama.[11] Through the female characters in *Jonah's Gourd Vine,* Hurston begins the historical and psychological development of the acclaimed model of female liberation found in the character of Janie Crawford. Through *Their Eyes,* Hurston defines herself as a woman in relation to the legacy of women who went before her and, most significantly, to those who, she imagined, would go after her.

These interlocking relationships between generations of women underscore the importance of establishing an audience of secondary witnesses when giving testimony. According to Laub, secondary witnesses are essential to documenting and thereby preventing the trauma from recurring: "For the testimonial process to take place, there needs to be a bonding, the intimate and total presence of an-*other*—in the position of one who hears. Testimonies are not monologues; they cannot take place in solitude."[12] By writing fiction, Hurston establishes a body of witnesses to receive her own personal testimony.

The significant correspondences between Hurston's life and the character of Janie suggests that *Their Eyes* is organized around an ethical imperative to give testimony to the traumas that Hurston both witnessed and experienced. One of the most striking correspondences is the similarity between the true-love relationship between Janie and Tea Cake and the older woman-younger man relationship Hurston had had with a man she only identifies as A.W.P. They first met in New York in 1931. He was a twenty-three-year-old college student and she a forty-year-old writer, anthropologist, and folklorist. In her autobiography, *Dust Tracks on a Road* (1942), Hurston describes his domination of her and the violence of their relationship. She explains that he was

> the master kind. All, or nothing, for him. The terrible thing was that neither could leave each other alone. . . . Let me seem too cordial with any male and something was going to happen. Just let him smile too broad at any woman, and no sooner did we get inside my

door than the war was on! One night . . . I slapped his face. That was a mistake. He was still smoldering from an incident a week old. A fellow had just met us on Seventh Avenue and kissed me on my cheek. Just one of those casual things, but it had burned up A. W. P. So I had unknowingly given him an opening he had been praying for. He paid me off then and there with interest. No broken bones, you understand, and no black eyes . . . Then I knew I was too deeply in love to be my old self. For always a blow to my body had infuriated me beyond measure. . . . But somehow I didn't hate him at all. . . . (186, 187)

Hurston goes on to say that when she wrote *Their Eyes,* she was getting over this affair and "tried to embalm all the tenderness of [her] passion for him" in the novel (*Dust Tracks* 188, 189). Her use of the word "embalm" is a telling choice for describing the end of a violent relationship; the relevance of her word choice becomes apparent in the fictional scene where Janie and Tea Cake's affair ends because she shoots him as he is about to attack her. Hurston also gives testimony to the violence of her relationship with A.W. P. through a beating that Janie receives from Tea Cake so that he can publicly assert ownership of her. In the same way that A.W.P. beat Hurston because another man may have shown some affection for her, Tea Cake explains that he "'didn't whup Janie 'cause *she* done nothin'. [He] beat her tuh show dem Turners who is boss'" (141). Further correspondence between Janie and Tea Cake's affair and Hurston and A.W.P.'s relationship appears in the postbeating intimacy between Janie and Tea Cake. Just as Tea Cake is described as having "petted and pampered [Janie] as if those two or three face slaps had nearly killed her" (140). In her autobiography, Hurston says that after A.W.P. beat her, they "were more affectionate than ever" (*Dust Tracks* 187).[13] Ultimately, *Their Eyes* reflects upon Hurston's own vulnerability to male domination. The text serves as a venue for testimony and affords her a place where she can design an ideal self in the form of the character Janie who speaks to other women about self-love and independence.

Testimony from the Margin

In addition to her own traumatic experiences, Hurston's varied and shifting positions as a writer, anthropologist, maid, product of Eatonville, and intellectual allowed her a privileged view of the world. Because her testimony speaks both for and against her own community, critics have often discussed her position in relation to the community. In her excellent essay, "Thresholds of Difference: Structures of Address in Zora Neale Hurston," Barbara Johnson explains that the intellectual act of representing African American folk life for critical analysis requires that Hurston transform the power of each relative position so that while she shifted between an insider/outsider relationship with her community

Hurston's work itself was constantly dramatizing and undercutting just such inside/outside oppositions, transforming the plane geometry of physical space into the complex transactions of discursive exchange. In other words, Hurston could be read not just as an *example* of the 'non-canonical' writer but as a commentator on the dynamics of any encounter between an inside and outside, any attempt to make a statement about difference.[14]

Similarly, in her 1997 publication *Women Intellectuals, Modernism and Difference,* Alice Gambrell sees Hurston's protean position as questioning

the hierarchy implicit in relations between a credentialized observer and her or his subjects: When Hurston played the dual role of observer and informant, for example, she occupied an anthropological border area in which constitutive distinctions between the familiar and the strange, the domestic and the alien, became crossed and blurred.[15]

In a similar examination to that of Gambrell and Johnson, Hazel Carby understands Hurston's position as enabling her to create a "fictional world that can mediate and perhaps resolve the tension that exists in the difference between the socially constructed identities of 'woman' and 'intellectual' and the act of representing the folk."[16] These critical observations of Hurston's exploratory movements along these social borders to mediate difference and cross boundaries begin an important theoretical discussion on the fluidity of subjectivity and its relative power.

Their discussions invite an analysis of the source of Hurston's displacement and relegation to the boundaries of her home community. Many have understood her position solely as a by-product of her career choice—anthropologist to her own rural, southern community. While her role as anthropologist certainly affected her relative status, Hurston's marginal position was not established as an adult. Rather, it began when she was still a child. Her sense of abandonment by her father and her mother's death must be understood as childhood traumas. It is because of these traumatic events that her works are ethically driven by the desire to give testimony.

Evidence attesting to the actual occurrence of specific traumatic events in Hurston's life is validated by their repetitive narration in Hurston's work and by the findings of her biographer, Robert Hemenway. While Hurston's autobiographical rendering of her ultimate mastery over trauma forms part of her own larger-than-life identity construction, her motivation to attempt such mastery stemmed from actual events discussed in Hurston's autobiography and in Robert Hemenway's biography of Hurston. These events include Hurston's portrayal of her bitter grandmother, Lucy's deathbed scene, Hurston's last talk with her dying mother, John's questionable reaction to Lucy's death, John's gross neglect of his children, John's long absences while her mother was alive, Lucy's injunction to jump at the sun, John's violent threats against her mother with a rifle, and Hurston's own violent relationship with A.W.P.

In her autobiography, *Dust Tracks on a Road,* Hurston describes her child-hood relationship with her father and maternal grandmother as wrought with vi-olent threats and rejections that marginalized her status within her own immedi-ate family. Describing her father's reaction to her birth, Hurston explains that her older sister "Sarah was his favorite child, but that one girl was enough. Plenty more sons, but no more girl babies to wear out shoes and bring in nothing"(19). She goes on to say that once she was born, her father had to put up with her; "he was nice about it in a way. He didn't tie [her] in a sack and drop [her] in the lake, as he probably felt like doing" (20). Hurston makes it very clear that her father's rejection of her is based on gender. Her grandmother's scorn, which is based on Hurston's childhood game of storytelling, links her gender-based rejection to hav-ing a speaking voice.[17] While her father was always threatening to "break [her will] or kill [her] in the attempt," her grandmother vacillated between wanting to "break [her] or kill [her]. Killing [her] looked like the best one . . . [since] all she was good for was to lay up and wet the bed and tell lies" (13, 53).

Hurston concluded that her grandmother and father rejected her because she was an aggressive female with a "brazenness [that] was unthinkable" (34). Her only source of encouragement and protection came from her mother, who acted as a buffer, "always standing between" Hurston and her father (13). After her mother's death, Hurston had no source of protection. Her position changed from marginalized family member to outcast. Sent to school in Jacksonville, she was, initially, "put to scrubbing down the stair steps every Saturday and sent to help clean up the pantry and do what [she] could in the kitchen after school" because her father refused to pay her bill. At the end of the school year, no one came to take Hurston home and eventually "a letter came. [Her father] said that the school should adopt [her]" (79). This final act of rejection confirms Hurston's status as insider/outsider in relation to her own family. Hurston demonstrates how her ad-venturous and outspoken form of femaleness was unacceptable to her father by contrasting her father's threats of violence against her with his reaction to her older sister. Sarah "was diminutive. . . . [Her father] delighted in putting the fin-est and the softest shoes on her dainty feet; . . . 'Dat's a switching little gal' he used to gloat. She had music lessons on the piano . . . When [Hurston] asked for music lessons [she] was told to dry up before he bust the hide on [her] back" (72, 73). Hurston's description of her position in relation to her family establishes her as an insider/outsider from birth. The threat of violence used to maintain Hurston's marginal status and the abusive reinscribing of her "difference" from the rest of the family had to be traumatic for her.

While she uses her fiction to give testimony to the traumatic origins of her outsider's position, her works can also be understood as tracing the "process of symbolic reproduction based on the traumatic experiences of those entering transi-tion[s], or liminal state[s]."[18] The originating source of Hurston's liminal position has often been displaced to her adult years as anthropologist; read as trauma testimony, the symbols she generates through her insider/outsider status take the form of disruptive, testifying fictions that create positive, liberating spaces.

Silence and Speech in Self-Division

The process of symbolic and literary reproduction as a form of testimony to the experience of trauma reveals answers to some of the ongoing critical questions concerning Zora Neale Hurston's characterization of Janie in her highly acclaimed novel, *Their Eyes Were Watching God* (1937). One of the most extensive critical discussions on *Their Eyes* debates the connection between Hurston's insider/outsider status and Janie's interior/exterior identities. A great deal of attention has been devoted to discussing what has been termed the figurative dimension, the authentic voice, and an anti-feminist gesture in *Their Eyes*. For example, Barbara Johnson argues that "self-difference" or fracture "authenticates" Janie's voice. Mary Helen Washington argues that Hurston's text is not as liberational as women may like to believe. By linking the appearance of Janie's divided consciousness to her decision to talk back to her husband, Washington concludes that "speech does not lead Janie to power, . . . but to self division and to further acquiescence in her status as object."[19]

Washington's reading of Janie's self-division leads to the conclusion that some critics have underrated the operative value of Janie's interior consciousness. In fact, Hurston makes a careful distinction between Janie's "prostrating," "shadows of herself" and the substantial "she herself" who "sat under a shady tree with the wind blowing through her hair" (73). The distinction between these two is vital, since the exterior, prostrating Janie acts out the limits of an identity imposed on her by her husband. Furthermore, reading *Their Eyes* as trauma testimony explains how Janie's self-division came about. The emergence of Janie's interior/exterior identities can only be understood in a traumatic frame where the continuity between the text as testimony and the text as a mechanism of survival becomes apparent.

I propose that Janie's interior/exterior existence gives voice to Hurston's insider/outsider status and demonstrates how the literary mediation between traumatic experience and social isolation attempts to rupture patterns of intergenerational trauma among women. Because "atrocities against women [were] grounded in a system that support[ed] them, which in fact encourage[d] [them]," there were few, if any, outlets for testimony during Hurston's lifetime.[20] Indeed, because Hurston is both descendent and victim of violent heterosexual relationships, she develops a female heroine born of her grandmother's, her mother's, and her own experiences. Like Hurston, Janie goes in search of love and ultimately finds that the truest form comes in the advice of the fictional representation of her mother, Lucy Potts Pearson: "'[D]on't love nobody better'n yo do yo'self'" (*Jonah's* 130). Hurston's persona, Janie, cannot immediately act on this advice; however, the testimonial drive that organizes *Their Eyes* ethically requires that secondary witnesses (in this case the reading public) follow the narrative and acknowledge that the heroine's stages of development are marked by traumatic events.

One of Janie's early traumatic experiences occurs as a result of being subjected to a loveless marriage, where the marriage vow forces her to make herself sexually available to a man from whom she is emotionally estranged. Her second stage of development results from the trauma of being in a much longer marriage where she is continually silenced and made to feel powerless. Finally, even in the idyllic love relationship with Tea Cake, Janie experiences the trauma of physical violence along with the persistent demand that, in order to experience love, men must be able to claim ownership of women. These traumas inscribe the interior and exterior spaces of Janie's existence. The power that Janie ultimately claims for herself emerges from her ability to give testimony.

In addition, Hurston's descriptions of clearly demarcated interior and exterior activity also serve as a key figure to identify the presence of trauma. In *Beyond the Pleasure Principle,* Freud suggests that "what is inside the psyche is a mediation of the outside through desire, repression, and so on. In trauma, there is an incomprehensible outside of the self that has already gone inside without the self's mediation."[21] Hurston's depiction of the interior/exterior space should be read as evidence of a traumatic split that supports the "notion of a dissociation of the psyche around the event—the splitting off of a 'traumatic memory'" from the rest of consciousness.[22]

This process of dissociation often leads to the birth of a new self whose identity is circumscribed by the traumatic experience. Hurston's ability to write from her own experience of trauma is, in itself, very telling since it enables her to transfer the story to others and thereby see herself in a different and more powerful way. As Dori Laub explains in his essay "Bearing Witness or the Vicissitudes of Listening," the "reexternalization of the event can occur and take effect only when one can articulate and *transmit* the story, literally transfer it to another outside oneself and take it back inside again."[23] Hurston's ability to create an ideal female persona in the character of Janie and to narrate the journey of this persona reflects her attempt to document the process of mediation between trauma and survival.

Hurston's textualization of her own trauma attempts to "undo the entrapment in a fate that . . . cannot be told, but can only be repeated."[24] By writing, she engages in "a therapeutic process—a process of constructing narrative, of reconstructing a history and essentially of *re-externalizing* [events]."[25] The character of Janie becomes the venue through which Hurston externalizes her own experiences and responds to her mother's and her grandmother's experiences. The difference between Janie's interior and exterior activity is that her exterior responses to an oppressive system of patriarchy are often through "recognition," or "discerning" her own identity as distinct from her grandmother's. Nanny's position as an ex-slave woman shapes her identity. Fearful of Janie's budding sexuality, Nanny insists that she marry old man Killicks and his "'oft mentioned sixty acres'" (21). Nanny sees this marriage as providing Janie protection against "'menfolks white or black makin' a spit cup outa [her]'" (20). After Janie marries Killicks, however, he begins to exert his domination over her. The clearest expression of his intent to dominate her emerges in his decision to buy a mule for her to plow with. She responds by walking out on him and his sixty acres. Janie's exterior response to his attempt to dominate her simultaneously recognizes and distinguishes her from Nanny who associates power and freedom with land and money.

Janie's interior responses are, by contrast, entirely focused on defining a new and more liberating self-enunciation. Throughout the novel, Jane's inside thoughts, her interior identity, seek to imbue meaning to a life that, without *new* enunciation, remains subject to male-centered evaluation. Her first demonstration of an interior search for self-definition comes after an argument where Killicks threatens to kill her with an ax:

> [Janie] turned from the door without answering, and stood still in the middle of the floor without knowing it. She turned wrongside out just standing there feeling. . . . she gave [Killicks's] speech a hard thought and placed it beside other things she had seen and heard . . . She wasn't even angry. Logan was accusing her of her mamma, her grandmama and her feelings. (32)

Consciously separating herself from the literal context of her foremothers, Janie, like Hurston, uses the distance that this separation allows her to explore alternative modes of existence where self-evaluation becomes critical.

For Hurston, the critical function of self-evaluation is particularly important in the context of her hometown, Eatonville, where "there were no discreet nuances of life [and] . . . all emotions were naked and nakedly arrived at" on the front porch of Joe Clark's store (*Dust Tracks* 46). In her autobiography, Hurston describes the men's porch talk as intriguing to her as a child. Although she was not allowed to listen, she often lingered long enough to hear the folk tales and the seemingly endless discussions that objectified women's bodies. In *Their Eyes,* she recreates the Eatonville store and its front porch. Janie's second husband, Jody Starks, owns the store; Hurston's restaging of the porch-front talk fests reveal Janie's exclusion from the conversations. Through this literary restaging, Hurston presents much of the male response to heterosexual relationships as so oppressive and controlling that those women on the receiving end of their philosophies are subject to psychic and/or physical trauma. The porch-front consensus on what to do with a wife who gets out of hand illustrates the extreme measures that men consider taking in order to dominate women. For example, when a woman goes against her husband's wishes and tries to get free store goods, one man exclaims "'if dat wuz mah wife . . . Ah'd kill her cemetery dead'" (74). After Jody dies, the desire to control Janie and her money encourage the town men to preach that "'uh woman by herself is a pitiful thing . . . Dey needs aid and assistance. God never meant 'em tuh try tuh stand by theirselves'" (90). When Janie returns to town after Tea Cake's death, the communal voice of the porch sees her as fragmented parts. They describe her "in a string of anecdotes, naming parts of her body— such as her 'great rope of black hair,' 'her pugnacious breasts,' 'her faded shirt and muddy overalls'—as parts standing for the whole."[26] The psychological impact of being reared within an environment of exclusion and objectification is apparent in Hurston's delivery of a heroine who undergoes a process of self-division as a mechanism of survival.

Owing the Space to Speak

When the men's porch talk turns toward issues of gender, women are consistently objectified and silenced. While *Their Eyes* renders speech an important part of Janie's quest, it is important to note that Janie's freest and most revealing speech occurs on her own porch; Hazel Carby points out that "critics often forget that Janie is a protagonist whose subject position is defined through class, that she can speak on a porch because she owns it."[27] The fact that Janie had to own a porch in order to speak from one undercuts the popular view that Hurston idealized the folk in her work and emphasizes the need for women to have an uncensored speaking place where testimony can occur.

Early in the novel, Hurston establishes the porch as the communal center where "crayon enlargements of life" are talked into view (50). The men of the town shape and color these enlargements in ways that are often oppressive to women. For example, Janie's initial arrival into town is

> described through the eyes and speech of the men on the front porch. Jody joins the men, but Janie is seen "through the bedroom window getting settled." Not only are Janie and the other women barred from participation in the ceremonies and rituals of the community, but they become objects of the sessions on the porch, included in the men's tale-telling as the butt of their jokes, or their flattery, or their scorn.[28]

Rather than idealizing the folk, Hurston uses the persona of Janie to reveal her own ambivalent view of Eatonville folklife.[29] The community is "indicted as a 'Mouth Almighty,' a powerful voice that lacks intellectual direction."[30] Hurston describes the town that greets Janie as made up of people who "made burning statements with questions, and killing tools out of laughs. It was mass cruelty. A mood come alive. Words walking without masters" (2). When Janie returns as an *experienced* speaking voice, she details

> the antagonistic relation between [herself], as a woman alone, and the folk as community. The community sits "in judgment" as . . . Janie walks through the town to enter her house. . . . In the opening chapter, oral language is represented as a "weapon" a means for the destruction and fragmentation of the self rather than a cultural form, which preserves a holistic personal and social identity. She has broken the boundaries of social convention and becomes the accused.[31]

Taking a revolutionary turn, Janie shifts her own position and becomes the accuser by questioning the community's right to judge her life from their positions of relative ignorance. She explains that "'talkin' don't amount tuh uh hill uh beans when yuh can't do nuthin' else'" (192). By speaking from her own porch, she establishes a platform of free expression, allowing her to transform the community's use of folkloric language as a weapon for patriarchal control into testimonial language used as an affirmation of female liberation.[32]

Traditionally, African American folklore transmits culturally acceptable social practices. A large number of the stories "concern themselves with social behavior. [T]hey are prologues to a pedagogic or moralizing peroration. [The] content may be adventure, humor, and entertainment, but the interpretation, whether explicit or implied, is serious."[33] The socially defined seriousness of the tale gives the speaker an authority much like the authority of any regional legislator. In her essay "Folklore and Music," Hurston defines folklore as a readily available tool for liberating expression by describing it as the "boiled-down juice of human living [and] not belong[ing] to any special time, place or people."[34]

Hurston's persistent critique of the patriarchal control of discourse in her own southern, rural community also appears in her autobiography, where she recalls the main ritual of Eatonville as occurring at Joe Clark's store: "[T]he heart and spring of the town, [m]en sat around the store on boxes and benches and passed this world and the next one through their mouths. The right and the wrong, the who, when and why was passed on, and nobody doubted the conclusions."[35] She contrasts this image of male legislative authority with the silent passivity of the women who "stood around there on Saturday nights . . . [to prove] to the community that their husbands were good providers."[36] Similarly, the oppressive nature and absolute authority of the men's porch talk appears in *Their Eyes* as the male community expresses the power to "break or kill" a wife if she cannot be controlled (74). The conversation goes on to validate violently enforced male domination and receives a majority sanction by four out of the five men present.

The storefront conversations take their tone and frame from the oral tradition of folklore. Contextualized within the easy setting of the porch, folklorically framed social conventions are transmitted casually. Men coming together during their leisure hours inscribe social conventions thereby creating a male-dominated venue for encoding terrifying messages that often serve to instill fear in women. The transmission of folktales and other forms of community prescriptives through male heads of households establish a type of dictatorship where men determine the form and content of the tale. The result is that, while folklore often serves as a medium for cautionary tales that benefit the community, it can also be used to reinforce patriarchal gender relations.

Hurston's attention to disrupting the patriarchal control of cultural practices began early in her life. In *Dust Tracks* she describes the Eatonville men "straining against each other in telling folk tales" while the hard-working "wives of the story-tellers [would yell] from the backyards for them to come and tote some water or chopwood . . . and never get a move out of the men" (47). Being a female child, Hurston was "naturally, not allowed to sit around there" (46). As an adult, Hurston creates a setting where women are allowed to tell their tales. Janie, her alter ego in *Their Eyes,* eventually owns a porch of her own, but even before that point in the novel, Hurston illustrates Janie's courage and determination to speak. Following the male dialogue on beating and killing uncontrollable women, Janie intercedes with a moral reminder that "'sometimes God gits familiar wid . . . womenfolks too and talks his inside business. He told [her] how surprised he was 'bout y'all turnin' out so smart after Him makin' yuh different; and how surprised y'all is goin' tuh be if you ever find out you don't know half as much 'bout us as you think you do. It's so easy tuh make yo'self out God Almighty when you ain't got nuthin' tuh strain agains but women and chickens'" (75). Janie first attempts to speak on the male-owned porch in defense of women, and she is silenced. She does not have free speech until she is on her own porch.

Through *Their Eyes,* Hurston alters the structure of folkloric cultural transmission as she had known it. She attains her goal not by eliminating the use of folklore but by granting women access to its power. Janie's self-owned porch and the tone of wisdom with which she delivers her own evaluation of life gives authority to Janie's concluding view of the world: "'[Y]ou got tuh *go* there tuh *know* there'" (192). Janie, Hurston's alter ego, retains the naturalizing dimensions of folkloric cultural transmission by maintaining the age-old tone of speech and the porch setting, but the speaker and the audience are radically female, and the story's content is shaped as testimony to trauma and survival.

Hurston's contrast of the male and female-owned porches articulates the potential for creating self-owned, self-defined spaces of female expression. In spite of this, a continuing debate surrounds the issues of silence in *Their Eyes.* After shooting Tea Cake, Janie appears in court, where she has to define her relationship with Tea Cake and explain the circumstances of his killing to a judging white community and the folk on the "Muck," who had been their friends and neighbors. During this courtroom scene, Hurston delivers Janie's testimony in a third-person omniscient voice. This scene has been the source of great debate over Janie's development. Critics such as Robert Stepto, Hazel Carby, and Mary Helen Washington have argued that the use of the third-person in this scene renders Janie silent. In light of this controversial debate, the most revealing source for understanding Janie's silences is the narrative course of *Their Eyes*. Janie's full, open-mouthed testimony constitutes the circular shape of the text and traces her return to the traumatic events that compel her to transmit her story to other women.

The novel opens and closes with Janie articulating her development into a fully realized, self-actualized woman. The verbal jousting, which she engages during her journey, only provides rehearsals that demonstrate her potential as an autonomous individual, a leader of women, and a mother of a testimonial tradition. For example, when she defends herself from public humiliation by verbally retaliating against Jody, she attacks his masculinity and tells him, "'when you pull down yo' britches you look like de change uh life'" (79). While this scene illustrates Janie's ability to defend herself against Jody's verbal degradation, she still suffers the trauma of violence and male domination of the worst kind; in response to her statement, Jody "struck Janie with all his might and drove her from the store" (80).

Janie's life with Tea Cake allows her to continue to develop her own voice—she "got so she could tell big stories herself"—but this in itself does not constitute autonomy. Even though Hurston presents Janie's adventurous life with Tea Cake as conducive for her to *begin* developing her own voice, violence limits her development. As Mary Helen Washington explains, the "most stunning silence occurs after Tea Cake beats Janie. The beating is seen entirely through the eyes of the male community, while Janie's reaction is never given."[37] In fact, the males in the community respond with an envy that is both gendered and racialized: "Tea Cake, you sho is a lucky man, . . . a person can see every place you hit her" (147). By extending her critique of heterosexual relationships to even the most idyllic love relationships, Hurston underscores the extent to which women are often violently subjugated in the name of love.

Hurston renders Janie's escape from male domination with a complexity that mirrors her own escape from her younger lover, A.W.P.[38] She uses the persona of Janie to express the conflicting duality of her own existence as an autonomous individual and, while with A.W.P., a violently dominated woman. Hurston's attempt to express this duality guides her through the process of translating trauma into text. Entwined with this act of testimony is an ethical drive requiring her to retain interpretive authority of her own trauma in order to, ultimately, revolutionize oppressive social and political systems. Indeed, within the context of her own narrative, Hurston achieves her aim by demonstrating how the latent aspect of trauma provides the necessary time and space that survivors need in order to interpret the traumatic event for themselves.

The psychically latent dimension of traumatic experience restricts the survivor's *immediate access* to the psychological resources necessary to organize and narrate the experience. Latency describes the period during which the effects of the experience are not apparent; Freud

> . . . describes trauma as the successive movement from an event to its repression to its return. . . . Since the traumatic event is not [fully] experienced as it occurs, it is fully evident only in connection with another place and in another time.[39]

Janie demonstrates this period of latency through her inability to give full testimony until she is away from the "Muck," "in another place and in another time." The sociopolitical aspect of Hurston's depiction of traumatically induced latency takes its power from Janie's narrative prowess on her own porch. In fact, the timing and the setting of her testimony confirm her authority to translate her own traumatic experience into a narrative that also operates as a social prescriptive. Janie, as a speaking subject and as a reflection of Hurston's persona, adds sustenance to Hurston's literary testimony to her own trauma. It is through the literary depiction of Janie's return that Hurston can holistically approach and evaluate her own experiences and obtain an authoritative form of communal transmission.

In their critical analyses of Janie's moments of silence and speech, Stepto, Carby, and Washington fail to take into account that Janie does not attain the power to tell her own story until *after* she kills the jealous and rabid Tea Cake. The timing of Janie's full testimony reflects the period of latency and demonstrates the narrative's effort to control the force of trauma. For Janie, Tea Cake has been "a glance from God" (106). He represented the love she had been searching for all her life. He manifested the "springtime bloom of the pear tree" (10, 11).[40] Still, he beats her. Janie never speaks of the beating, but on the very next occasion that Tea Cake threatens her, she shoots him. Using the metaphor of mad-dog rabidity to describe his violent heterosexual jealousy, Hurston places only one chapter between Tea Cake's initial beating of Janie and her shooting of him. Hurston uses this thirteen-page chapter to contextualize Tea Cake's contraction of rabies by describing a storm wherein he is bitten by a rabid dog. The rabies are manifested in Tea Cake's irrational jealousy that acts upon his "disordered mind" in a way that makes him "jealous and [wanting] to scare her" (182). When Janie follows the doctor's orders and does not sleep in the same bed with him, he becomes irrational and "level[s] a gun at [her] breast. . . . Tea Cake's suffering brain was urging him on to kill" (183). By depicting jealousy and violence as an incurable, maddening, and life-threatening condition, Hurston reflects upon her father's domination of her mother, and the control that A.W.P. exerted over her. When Janie kills Tea Cake in the novel, Hurston "embalms all the tenderness of her passion" for A.W. P. and gives testimony to the trauma of the violence in that relationship (*Dust*

Tracks 188, 189). As with her alter ego, Janie, Hurston's testimony to the violence of her relationship comes after a period of latency. *Their Eyes,* the fictionally framed testimony to her experience, does not appear until seven months after leaving the United States on a Guggenheim Fellowship and ending her affair with A.W. P.[41]

Similarly, because she is traumatized and still within a period of latency, Janie cannot speak for herself in the courtroom scene. Instead of Janie's voice, a third-person omniscient voice navigates through Janie's consciousness, and, with startling familiarity, explains that she shot Tea Cake because he "couldn't come back to himself until he had got rid of that mad dog that was in him and he couldn't get rid of that dog and live. He had to die to get rid of the dog" (187).

The authority and presence of the third-person omniscient narrator also serves as Hurston's narrative figuration of the spilt in consciousness that often accompanies traumatic experience. Hurston uses the narrator to reveal Janie's inner desires while she physically describes Janie sitting "like a lump" in the courtroom (188). The discontinuity between Janie's inner desires and her physical stagnation, along with the lack of her own voice, supports the "notion of a dissociation of the psyche around the event—the splitting off of a 'traumatic memory'" from the rest of consciousness that is described earlier in this chapter.[42]

Often this dissociation of the psyche—this splitting off—leads to the birth of a new self whose identity is circumscribed by the traumatic experience. Not until the period of latency is past does Janie emerge as a new woman who can fully tell her own story. The autobiographical dimension of this novel suggests that "Hurston has motivated her narrative . . . to act out her rage against male domination and to free Janie, a figure for herself, from all men."[43] Hurston's attempt to master and manipulate both traumatic temporality and the splitting of consciousness helps her to develop the criteria for becoming a speaking female subject. Together, the context of the self-owned porch and the latent timing of her persona's translation of traumatic experience infuse the narrative with a female-centered model of production. This model effectively establishes lines of kinship among women that redefine the act of mothering.

Lines of kinship among black women writers have been described as emerging from a "common scene recurring in . . . [black women's fiction] [where] . . . women (usually two) gather together in a small room to share intimacies that can be trusted only to a kindred female spirit."[44] Hurston's depiction of Janie and Pheoby sharing the intimacy of Janie's testimony reflects the close ties and deep trust existing between the two women. Hurston establishes the intimate relation between the two by having Janie remind Pheoby that "we been kissin'-friends for twenty years; [so]. . . . mah tongue is in mah friend's mouf" (6, 7). Because the scene is between two women, the reproductive aspect of this intimacy often goes unnoticed.

Giving Birth to Testimonial Narrative

In *Their Eyes,* the only detailed discussion of sexual reproduction comes from Janie's grandmother, Nanny. Nanny's motherhood is the direct result of her master's coercion, while Janie is the product of her mother's rape (17, 19); hence, both Janie and her mother result from violently enforced heterosexual encounters. Perhaps for this reason, Hurston renders a heroine whose three marriages, which also hold varied levels of violence, produce no biological children. Unlike her grandmother or her mother, Janie's generation of women has a wider range of life choices. She is neither a slave woman nor a second-generation slave woman. Janie's life in an all-black town, mobility, and cultural literacy expand her horizons. While Hurston's heroine inherits the legacy of intergenerational trauma from Nanny and her mother, she does not fully repeat the entrapment of patriarchal domination by producing biological children with men who claim ownership over her body. Through Janie, Hurston renders a liberated female who reproduces descendants outside the boundaries of patriarchy.

The violence associated with Janie's three marriages has impregnated her with the seed of alterity that implicitly rejects reproduction of and with males in favor of self-reproduction. The psychic split that impairs Janie's speech in the courtroom signals the birth of another self—a consciousness articulated by the desire to testify to the experience of violent and oppressive heterosexual relationships. When Janie returns home, it is Pheoby, her "kissin'-friend," who correctly identifies as a descendant the woman that Janie's experiences produced: "[Y]ou sho looks *good.* You looks like youse yo' own daughter. . . . Even wid dem overhalls on, you shows yo' womanhood" (4).

Heterosexual relationships often produce children who, on a variety of levels, bind the man, the woman, and their history together. In contrast, Hurston renders the violence of Janie's heterosexual relationships as producing a split in consciousness that facilitates an alternate form of reproduction. Janie births her own daughter; this daughter-descendent is her speaking self. *Their Eyes Were Watching God* employs

> a "narrative strategy of the multiple individual,". . . . her power is articulated in and continued through a community that is formed in direct answer to the claims of love and romance. Not only is the traditional heterosexual couple supplanted as emphasis of the action, but it is replaced by interchangeable versions of the same-sex couple: mother and daughter, sisters, lovers, narrator and audience. . . . Perhaps most significantly, the mother-daughter relation is continuously transformed.[45]

Hurston not only transforms the mother-daughter relationship, but she goes much further by expanding the boundaries of female reproduction. Her depiction of Janie suggests that a traumatic split of consciousness can, eventually, function as a reproductive source for a new and powerful identity, which is shared with other females in the community.

> The collaborative model of maternal influence suggests a subversively extended family romance, in which the mother as co-creator is simultaneously parent of the writer and her lover or spouse. Most disruptively, for the absolute status of all these role definitions, she may even become the daughter of her own daughter.[46]

Hurston's self-reflection, Janie, models women's ability to give birth to the next generation of women without heterosexual love—without having to grant male access to, or power over, their bodies. In fact, the emergent speaking woman who "looks like [Janie's] own daughter," has full control of her own text only after she has murdered Tea Cake—her rabidly jealous lover. Her ability to rebirth herself as her own daughter is contingent upon her ability to love herself more than she loves him.[47] The self-articulated claim to her own voice is prefigured by her ability to kill off a violent and rabid love affair.

As *Their Eyes Were Watching God* demonstrates, in order for women to heal psychologically from the trauma of patriarchal domination, they must produce bodies of testimony. Hurston's desire to promote social changes stems from her own personal experiences. The impact of her traumatic experiences dictates the direction of her work and reveals that Hurston was often "caught in the dilemma of how she might both govern and exploit the autobiographical impulses that partially direct her [texts]."[48] *Their Eyes Were Watching God*, and her first novel, *Jonah's Gourd Vine,* establish an important historical, cultural, and experiential line of kinship for black female novelists writing later in the twentieth century. Ultimately, these texts become maternal sites that allow an autonomous form of reproduction that instigates the disruption of social orders.

CHAPTER FOUR

Sites of Rupture in *Dust Tracks on a Road*

> When I have been made to suffer or when I have been made happy by others, I have known
> that individuals were responsible for that, and not races. All clumps of people turn out to
> be individuals on close inspection.
> —Zora Neale Hurston, *Dust Tracks on a Road*

Published in late November 1942, Hurston's autobiography, *Dust Tracks on a Road,* was written after her publisher, Bertram Lippincott, suggested that she write her life story. She wrote the first draft in the summer of 1941 and spent the rest of the year adhering to Lippincott's demand that she rewrite those sections of the book containing criticism against America's role in international politics and warfare.[1] Since the publication of *Dust Tracks,* critics have used it as a resource for evaluating the ideological basis of Hurston's other works.

In fact, her autobiography has received more negative criticism than any of her other books. As Hemenway points out, it has been used by "those who . . . wish to criticize her fiction, [by] claim[ing] that *Dust Tracks* shows how her folksiness eventually became both style and substance."[2] In his 1942 review, for example, Arna Bontemps concludes that Hurston's autobiography proves that she "deals very simply with the more serious aspects of Negro life—she ignores them."[3] In addition, in 1943, critic Harold Preece writes that *Dust Tracks* is "the tragedy of a gifted mind, eaten up by egocentrism [and] fed on the patronizing admiration of the dominant white world."[4] This critique continues Preece's earlier attack in the December 1936 edition of *Crisis:* He accuses Hurston of devoting her "literary ability to recording the legendary amours of terrapins" and explains that the resentment toward Hurston by her black peers stems from this devotion because it is viewed as the efforts of a "literary climber."[5] Preece's comments reflect the sentiments of many who were angered by Hurston's refusal to write within the lines of racial tragedy. Ironically, Hurston received a $1,000 award for *Dust Tracks* from the John Ainsfield Awards in Racial Relations because of the book's concern with racial problems. Even Alice Walker, Hurston's literary descendant, notes that while *Dust Tracks* was Hurston's most commercially successful book, "it rambles on from one pose to another, sometimes boasting about her achievements and at all times deftly avoiding self-revelation."[6]

Most of the critical complaint about *Dust Tracks* emerges from its paradoxical construction. Robert Hemenway notes that *Dust Tracks* is "an autobiography at war with itself."[7] He explains the textual contradictions as resulting from the large amounts of editing required by Lippincott:

> The manuscript version of *Dust Tracks* displays a more self-assured, irreverent, and politically astute figure than the Zora Neale Hurston of the published book. It also exhibits some of the same disorganization and contradiction, but this is largely overcome by a tough-minded, let-the-chips-fall-where-they-may attitude.[8]

The autobiography that ended up being published still retains a tough-minded tone and, at times, a Herculean strength. The political commentary remains astute, but this latter section of the text does not explain the "textual ambivalence and contradictions aris[ing] out of the confusion of voice, that [is] in the autobiography from the first."[9] Her biographer correctly defines this confusion of voice as reflecting her "search for an appropriate voice for the post-Eatonville Zora Neale Hurston."[10] Furthermore, as Hemenway suggests, it is only "in the first portion of *Dust Tracks* [that] Hurston produce[s] a traditional autobiography; she creates a sense of the shared life she knew in Eatonville as a black child."[11] Like Hemenway, Alice Walker also concedes that the most forthright portions of the text are the sections on Hurston's childhood. These sections, Walker explains, "provide a fairly clear view of Hurston as a child, and [are] especially useful for detailing her relationships with her mother, father, and Eatonville."[12] Hurston presents an autobiography that *seemingly* gives limited access to her inner self and her true identity. However, because of the precise detailing of her most important relationships, those she had with her mother, father, and the town of Eatonville, and because of Hemenway's authentication of her Eatonville voice, along with Alice Walker's "clear view" of Hurston's childhood, the deathbed scene, the troubled relationship with her father, and her sense of alienation from her family, these aspects are understood as comprising a factual account of Hurston's early life.

Additional evidence of the factual basis of these events appears in Hurston's decision to devote three-fifths of *Dust Tracks* to chronicling her movement from childhood toward college and a career.[13] The autobiography traces Hurston's movement from childhood to adulthood by employing a repetition that is often used in testimonial literature; typically, the repetition creates a "textual itinerary of recurring words [and] figures" within the frame of the traumatic experience.[14] In

Hurston's case, the "textual itinerary" repeatedly leads us to the site of her mother's death. The deathbed scene appears in *Jonah's Gourd Vine, Seraph on the Suwanee,* and in *Dust Tracks,* where she not only revisits the deathbed scene but also details her psychological response to the event.[15] Another recurring site of trauma is the violence and dominance associated with her father as evidenced in her depiction of him in *Jonah's Gourd Vine* and in *Dust Tracks.* In *Dust Tracks,* Hurston's discussion of her father's violently enforced dominance and her mother's death allows us to understand the text as a self-defining work that is intricately tied to her attempt to gain mastery over these central traumas of her life.

Returning to the Site of Trauma

Because she attempts to master these traumas through literary discourse, Hurston's autobiography sits well within the broader tradition of African American autobiographical writing.[16] Black autobiography is often concerned with testifying about surviving the collective trauma of violence and disfranchisement, which are often veiled in racist and sexist pathologies. In his introduction to *On Bearing Witness,* Henry Louis Gates explains that black autobiography emerged out of the "black individual's [desire] to create herself or himself in words":

> "I write myself, therefore I am" could very well be taken as the motto of "the [black] race" in this country. The perilous journey from object to subject is strewn with black autobiographies. . . . In African American tradition, it appears the channel of existence had to be transgressed by one's self. . . . One crossed that abyss by an act of individual will, positing humanity, selfhood, and citizenship with the stroke of a pen.[17]

In similar fashion, Hurston's *Dust Tracks* demonstrates how her "act[s] of individual will" help her to negotiate between the traumatic experiences of her life and the desire to contain and therefore to define the significance of those experiences.[18] Although the traumas of Hurston's life include rejection by her father, her violent love affair with A.W. P., and living under the rule of Jim Crow, the central trauma of her life was the death of her mother.[19]

Hurston's mother, Lucy, provided her with encouragement, education, and protection. According to *Dust Tracks,* it was Lucy Hurston who "carried [her] past long division in arithmetic, and parsing sentences in grammar" (12). In the text, Hurston describes her mother as exhorting the "children at every opportunity to 'jump at de sun.' [They] might not land on the sun, but at least they would get off the ground" (13). During the many occasions that Hurston's father attempted to "squinch [her] spirit," her mother would stand between them and claim Zora as exclusively hers. Hurston describes Lucy's special attention to her as stemming from the desire to foster her daughter's independent spirit and to reduce the chance of her "turning out to be a mealy-mouthed rag doll by the time [she] got grown" (13). Warning her husband to "leave [Zora] alone," she claimed sole authority to "tend to her when . . . she need[ed] it" (13, 14). After her mother's death, Hurston found herself unhinged and rootless; she was "shifted from house to house of relatives and friends" (85). Hurston's autobiography reflects her attempt to anchor herself somehow to the realities of traumatic experiences that had caused her to feel castoff from the rest of the world.

When her publisher, Bertram Lippincott, suggested to Hurston that she write an autobiography she agreed initially to write it, but she came to resist the project; she claimed that she "did not want to write it at all, because it is too hard to reveal one's inner self, and still there is no point in writing that kind of book unless you do."[20] Hurston's concern introduces the paradoxical elements of autobiography and testimonial writing. While the author feels a drive to reveal, she also resists laying bare an often unrecognizable inner self. In many instances of trauma testimony, "the imperative to tell . . . is inhibited by the impossibility of telling."[21] Because the autobiographical form demands a linear unfolding of the subject's life, it lends itself to the tense negotiations that occur as a result of the trauma survivor's simultaneous compulsion toward and resistance to testimony.

The interest of autobiographers, as Paul de Man makes clear in "Autobiography as De-Facement," is to "move from cognition to resolution and to action, from speculative to political and legal authority—with autobiography, as with the development of the unconscious, as with the structure of language used to write autobiography, there is an impulse to create a unified narrative."[22] de Man's apt description of the autobiographical movement toward a unified narrative takes a slightly different shape when the autobiographer is a trauma survivor. The survivor does not begin the process of producing a self-defining narrative from a point of full cognition. Because trauma results from a consciousness-rupturing event, the compulsion to create a unified narrative is linked to the survivor's need to make *cognitively* known those aspects of the event that, at the time, were too overwhelming to fully comprehend. In addition, the writer satisfies the impulse to unity by a process of repetition. Because of this process of repetition, Hurston's texts appear on a generational continuum in a setting that is never far away from home. They begin with *Jonah's Gourd Vine,* continue with *Their Eyes Were Watching God,* and culminate in retrospection through *Dust Tracks.* Each text revisits and revises her family's and her own relative position regarding heterosexual relationships, death, and violence against women. Both Sigmund Freud and Pierre Janet understood that the

> crucial factor that determines the repetition of trauma is the presence of mute, unsymbolized, and unintegrated experiences: "[A] sudden and passively endured trauma is relived repeatedly, until a person learns to remember simultaneously the effect and cognition associated with the trauma through access to language." This process, inherent to trauma,

links trauma to autobiographical literary tradition in that there is a fictive element to all
language and particularly to the construction of one's own historical identity.[23]

Hurston's writing of *Dust Tracks* reflects her attempt to gain mastery over the traumatic elements of her personal history. The disunity of the text itself exemplifies
how trauma disrupts her early self-consciousness, making the linear narration of
her identity development impossible.

Whereas critics have noted Hurston's tendency, in her autobiography, to "unfold the structures of meaning—[through] the cultural 'topics' that are discussed
chapter by chapter (history, geography, mythology, and so forth)" anthropologi-
cally, it is important to understand that Hurston's career as an anthropologist
began with her family's rejection of her and her exile from Eatonville.[24] Zora left
home as the direct consequence of her mother's death. The life she describes in
Dust Tracks, without the sheltering arms of her mother, is one of poverty and despair. Her immediate departure to school in Jacksonville with no financial support
meant that she had to scrub stairs to support herself (77). After the school rejects
her, and after her father suggests that they adopt her, she returns to Eatonville
where she is shifted from house to house, able to go to school only erratically
(85).[25] At home she senses that "she was not comfortable to have around"; after her
mother's death, she explains that "strange things must have looked out of [her]
eyes like Lazarus after his resurrection" (86). While Hurston's independent nature
and her father's rejection of her had always set her apart from the rest of her family, this period of her life firmly places her "in a world of vanished communion
with her kind" (43). This juncture of her life firmly delineates the insider/outsider
position that eventually made Hurston's anthropological "spy glass" so effective.

While the death of Hurston's mother forms the central trauma of her early
life, during her childhood her father's rejection of her also played a pivotal role in
developing the critical distance that an insider/outsider position inherently requires. The impact that Hurston's father-daughter relationship had on her forma-
tive years emerges in her repetitive returns to specific incidents that Hurston continually tries to come to terms with through her testimonial writing. As discussed
in chapter 1, *Jonah's Gourd Vine* presents the persona of her father, John Pearson,
as the stagnant product of historical determinism. His inability to learn from his
experiences condemns him to a transient life. In *Their Eyes,* Hurston completely
erases the need for paternal influence and delivers a persona of herself that produces her own descendants through the act of testimony.[26] In *Dust Tracks on a
Road,* Hurston describes the relationship between her parents as, a "relationship
informed by insidious trauma," a term coined by Laura S. Brown.

Brown defines incidents of insidious trauma as the "secret experiences that
women encounter in the interpersonal realm and at the hands of those [they]
love and depend upon."[27] She uses the work of her colleague, Maria Root, to call

attention to the "effects of oppression that are not necessarily overtly violent or threatening to bodily well-being at the given moment but that do violence to the soul and spirit."[28] The psychic violence that Hurston saw at work in her parents' marriage appears in the *Jonah's Gourd Vine* version of her mother's death when Lucy explains to her daughter that "'uh person kin be killed without bein' stuck a blow'" (130). Hurston expresses her sense of her mother's unhappiness in *Dust Tracks* as well. On two occasions, in the context of discussing her parents' relationship, she states: "I know that my mother was very unhappy" (10, 66). Testimony to threats of physical violence also appear in both texts. In *Jonah's Gourd Vine*, Hurston describes a jealous rage where John promises Lucy that "'if [she] ever start out de door tuh leave [him] . . . [he] means tuh blow [her] heart out and hang fuh it'" (111). In *Dust Tracks*, Hurston revisits the scene when she states that "on two occasions [she] heard [her] father threaten to kill [her] mother if she ever started towards the gate to leave him" (10).

The repetition of these scenes in both texts establishes Hurston's view of John Hurston as a failed husband. Her loyalty and sympathy for her mother force her to condemn him. She condemns him also for his failure as a father. After her mother's death, his failure as a father allowed him to treat Hurston and her siblings as if they were "in his way" (*Dust Tracks* 82). They were left in "ragged, dirty clothes, [with] hit-and-miss meals. The four older children were definitely gone for good. One by one, [Hurston] and the three younger ones were shifted to the homes of [her] Mama's friends" (*Dust Tracks* 82). Hurston goes on to explain the family's breakdown as almost inevitable because of John Hurston's inability to accomplish any task without Lucy's prodding. In a tone of bland resignation she comments on the disbursement of the Hurston children as inevitable to a man that was comfortable putting "his potentialities to sleep [to] be happy in the laugh of the day. [A man who] lived in ease" (*Dust Tracks* 66, 82). Hurston's home life had taught her that it took much more than ease to feed and clothe seven children. Hurston complains that she had never been told why her father "was away from home for months at time," but one of the consequences was that often there "would be no fresh meat in the house" (*Dust Tracks* 19, 20).

According to the events detailed in *Dust Tracks*, John Hurston's failure as a husband and father placed a tremendous burden on Lucy Hurston during her life. After her death, his failures became another source of trauma for the children who were left to fend for themselves. Zora returns to her mother's deathbed in both *Jonah's Gourd Vine* and *Dust Tracks*; in each text, she returns to the failures of her father and condemns him for his role in facilitating her exile from her family. In the midst of her grief, he put her up for adoption, failed to offer financial support for her education, and shuffled her from place to place until, with few options left, she left home.

After leaving home, Hurston devoted her life work to attempting to right the wrong of an event that permanently altered her relation to the world. Her persistent retelling constitutes a reenactment, a staging of the trauma through narrative departures and returns from what was, according to her own description, a psychically rupturing event that altered her consciousness to such an extent that she had a sense of being able to "walk by [her own] corpse. [She] could smell it and feel it" (86). Psychic trauma results from a breach in the human barrier against stimuli. The event comes as a shock to an unprepared victim. The lack of preparedness produces an experience of lost time; this experience establishes the temporal nature of the psychic breach. The event or death comes too soon, and the survivor's returning to, or restaging of the event constitutes their return to self as Other—both familiar and unrecognizable.[29] Through her description of the event and the frame of preparedness that she establishes for her testimony, Hurston's autobiographical return to the scene of her mother's death exemplifies significant elements of trauma testimony.

The Structure of Testimony

Dust Tracks consists of sixteen short chapters that include impersonal commentaries on black and white America, politics, a list of people she knew, and even a creative description of how Eatonville came into being. The span of its two hundred and nine pages reveals relatively little intimate information about post-Eatonville Hurston. The most detailed and intimate section is chapter 6, entitled "Wandering," where Hurston testifies to the trauma she experiences through her mother's death.

Interestingly, before giving testimony to this event, Hurston uses chapter 4, "Inside Search," to describe a series of twelve visions she claimed to have had as a child. Through these visions, Hurston foretells the hardships of her life. Understood as a testimonial project, which attempts to master the effect of trauma, this section on prophetic visions allows Hurston to prepare herself for the upcoming testimony in chapter 6. Part of becoming psychically prepared for restaging the death scene that she writes two chapters later involves depicting herself as extraordinarily powerful in all aspects of life. She characterizes herself as stronger than other females; [she] "discovered that [she] was extra strong by playing with other girls near [her] age. [She] had no way of judging the force of [her] playful blows" (29). Instead of engaging in lady-like play, "dolls caught the devil around [her]"; she preferred the masculine warrior-type heroes from Greek mythology. Hurston describes the novels that depict the lives of feminine females as "thin books about this and that sweet girl who gave up her heart to Christ and good works. Almost always they died from it, preaching as they passed. I was utterly indifferent to their deaths" (39). Rejecting the passivity of traditional female heroines, Hurston models herself after decidedly masculine heroic figures with god-like strength; "Hercules moved [her] most . . . [she] resolved to be like him" (39).

Hurston's concern with presenting a Herculean, larger-than-life image of infallibility continued throughout her life to such an extent that her biographer refers to it as an "obsess[ion] with the fear that she might be found to engage in self-pity."[30] The sequence of her autobiography establishes a self-alignment with god-like heroes, allowing her to reduce the impact of the upcoming traumatic event. By establishing herself as an indomitable spirit, she infuses the chronology of her narrative with a cognitive awareness of the trauma ahead. Her heroic ability to "stretch [her] limbs in some mighty struggle" renders an image of Hurston as a potent warrior figure able to overcome all of life's obstacles (41). The logistical placement of the visions before the death scene reflects her attempt to master her own trauma. By claiming that these visions gave her "a preview of things to come," Hurston creatively provides a set of circumstances that, retrospectively, equip her with the emotional preparation she needs in order to revisit her mother's deathbed.[31] Hurston's design of a prepared frame for her approach to the death scene is in keeping with Freud's findings concerning repetitive returns to traumatic sites; he found that repetitive returns to the event is a "psychological response to an unexpected trauma; survivors . . . revisit the event . . . and make themselves master of the situation that they were unprepared for in reality."[32]

Using a heroic veneer, Hurston is able to examine, once again, the split structure of her own identity.[33] At the very beginning of the "Inside Search," she explains that "people are prone to build a statue of the kind of person that it pleases them to be. And few people want to be forced to ask themselves: 'What if there is no me like my statue?'" (26). The statement reflects Hurston's effort to fashion a monumental exterior persona, and the question, "What if there's no me like my statue?" speaks to Hurston's sense of an alien interiority; her answer reflects a discontinuity and stands in stark contradiction to the artistic mastery she exerts over her external image. Her inability to fully answer her own question leads her to state that what remains when there is no "[you] like [your] statue" is fear. Far from mastering her trauma, she can only suggest that "the thing to do is to grab the broom of anger and drive off the beast of fear"(26). Indeed, this chapter of *Dust Tracks* serves to "drive off the beast of fear" by laying the groundwork for her return to the moment of her mother's death. She uses her retrospective position and her gifts as writer and anthropologist to design a psychologically prepared and, therefore, safe return to her mother's deathbed.

At the time of her mother's death, Hurston's ability to translate and express the totality of her emotional experience into language was impaired by the trauma. Retrospectively, she tries to minimize this loss of translation by anticipating the psychic rupture through these compensatory visions. By fictionalizing this segment of her history and retrospectively situating it at a strategic point in her narrative, Hurston becomes the creator of her own temporal rupture. Her need to give testimony through a veil of preparedness is driven by the need to master an impossible event—her mother's death. The visions allow her to use imaginary foreknowledge to buffer and displace the pain of the actual experience. Similarly, in *Beyond the Pleasure Principle,* Sigmund Freud discusses the potential effects of foreknowledge; he notes a distinct "difference between [psychological] systems that are unprepared and systems that are well prepared through being hypercathected."[34]

Writing this autobiographical testimony thirty-four years after the event, Hurston revisits the traumatic scene directly—not through a persona. Establishing psychic preparedness prior to giving testimony is vital to her because testimony to trauma always involves a re-wounding of the survivor.[35] Imagining that she had foreknowledge, Hurston writes, "I had knowledge before its time. I knew my fate. I knew that I would be an orphan and homeless. I knew that while I was still helpless, that the comforting circle of my family would be broken, and that I would have to wander cold and friendless until I had served my time" (42). The narrative voice of this passage reflects the continuation of Hurston's self-defined heroism. As part of the production of these visions, she presents her knowing in a calm tone of infinite wisdom. The heroic memory of herself is linked closely to the memory of her unheroic inability to fulfill the deathbed promises made to her mother:

> I was not to let them take the pillow from under Mama's head until she was dead. The clock was not to be covered, nor the looking glass. She trusted me to see to it that these things were not done. I promised her as solemnly as nine years could do that I would see to it. What years of agony that promise gave me. (62)[36]

Together, her heroic and unheroic memories produce a textual wavering that, in testimony, typically "responds to the movement of the narrative, which tells two stories at once, one of life and one of death."[37] While *Dust Tracks* celebrates Hurston's many journeys and the sheer "pleasure of sunrises blooming out of oceans," it also confesses her own sense of failure. She admits to having "given [her]self more harrowing pain than anyone else. . . . No one else can inflict the hurt of faith unkept" (254). The first and most devastating act of unkept faith in Hurston's life stems from her inability to fulfill the promises she made on the day that Lucy Hurston died. Hurston's sense of failure, combined with the death experience, establishes a site of trauma, which permanently alters her perceptions of the world around her. In her mind, even nature condemns her unworthiness; after the death, she describes the "sun [going] down on purpose to flee away from [her]" (65). Her failed promise is part of the traumatic event that binds mother and daughter together.

Hurston's "sun" imagery and its escape from her at the death scene is important in relation to her mother, who always encouraged her to "jump at de sun" (*Dust*

Tracks 13). Hurston consistently uses the horizon and sun imagery as symbols of attainment in her work. Their repeated presence reflects her drive to reclaim her lost mother and fulfill her promises.[38] Sun images appear, for example, in the final scene of *Their Eyes* when Hurston's persona, Janie Crawford, imagines her dead lover with "the sun for a shawl" and she "pull[s] in her horizon like a great fish net" (193). Similar use of the sun also appears in *Seraph on the Suwanee.* The main protagonist, Arvay, obeys the sun, and, in three instances, the horizon and sun images shape what "the big light [tell] her to do . . . [each time,] she made the sun welcome to come on in" (352). In *Jonah's Gourd Vine,* the persona of her mother, Lucy, gives "jump at de sun" encouragement to her husband, John (95), and in the last line of *Dust Tracks,* Hurston claims to have "touched the four corners of the horizon" (255). The final lines of these works demonstrate Hurston's inscription of her mother's powerful presence made visible through sun imagery.

While Claudia Tate's analysis of the textual placement of these images and their relationship to Hurston's mother does not define, as I do, Hurston's persistent return to her mother as a response to trauma, she adds to this discussion by concluding that each text

> complete[s] the impossible trip to the horizon so as to greet the sun at its origination and destination . . . represent[ing] the desire to recover the mother lost to her in death. . . . the recurring projections of such a journey throughout her works signal sites of desire in Hurston's writings. In addition, Freud's "Theme of the Three Caskets" (1913) identifies the place where textual pleasure is most intense—its closure: Here the narrative anticipates both gratifying and terminating desire.[39]

Although, as Tate observes, Hurston's recurring sun imagery anticipates gratification, her desire is never satisfied. Instead, Hurston's repetitive use of sun imagery to connect her to her lost mother signals the extent to which she was not only traumatized by the loss of her mother but also how she was equally traumatized by having to survive without her. Ultimately, the insistent narrative returns to her mother inform and shape the ethical imperatives that undergird her work.

Hurston's repetitive return to the death scene demonstrates the close relationship between trauma and survival. While the initial trauma occurs when she witnesses her mother's death, her compulsive returns demonstrate that it is not "only the moment of the event, but of the passing out of it that is traumatic; that survival itself, in other words, can be a crisis."[40] A common symptom of the crisis of survival appears in the form of a traumatic split that characterizes traumatic occurrences. The temporality of this "fundamental dislocation . . . is both testimony to the event and to the impossibility of its direct access."[41] Characters who undergo self-division repeatedly appear in Hurston's work, and, in her autobiography, she describes a similar self-division as a direct consequence of her relation to her mother's death.

In *Dust Tracks*, Hurston prefaces her crisis of survival by describing herself as "like other children in that death, destruction and other agonies were never meant to touch her"(26). Her self-alignment with normalcy and "other children" is sharply contrasted by the crisis of surviving an encounter with death that she says, "caused me to agonize over that moment for years to come . . . my thoughts would escape occasionally from their confines and stare me down" (64). In this description of herself, Hurston references the central trait of a psychic split. In this instance, the psychic split occurs because of a death that, as she says, "changed a world. That is, the world that had been built out of [Mama's] body and her heart" (65). Describing the self-division and subsequent alienation that signals her crisis of survival, Hurston locates the site but not the exact process of her traumatic split. She explains in general terms that it was "life [that] picked me up from the foot of Mama's bed and my feet in strange ways" (64). Transformed at the foot of her mother's deathbed, Hurston is no longer "like other children." Her feet, now set in "strange ways," mark the birth and the journey of a new individual who, at that "hour began [her] wanderings. Not so much in geography but in time. Then not so much in time as in spirit" (65). Subsequently, the duality of *Dust Tracks* as a narrative that tells the story of a life and the story of a death is made literal in Hurston's testimony to her own psychic split.

A Journey Through Loss

As I have argued, Hurston's "wanderings" are, to a great extent, directed and mediated by the loss of her mother. Finding a "jagged hole where [her] home used to be," Hurston explains that she was "forever shifting" (69, 86). She takes her direction from an ethical drive to fulfill her promises to her mother and live up to her mother's expectations; as Tate aptly notes, "together guilt and grief transform [Hurston's] ambition into reparations—works in honor of the mother. They preserve the mother's voice."[42] Extending this notion, I suggest Hurston's attempt both to preserve and to honor her mother's voice produced the first African American female anthropologist who, by virtue of that profession, is in the business of preserving and transmitting cultural forms of experience. Her female-centeredness and her persistent critique of patriarchal dominance over women can be understood as her desire to offer reparations to not only her mother, but to all women who went before her. While at her mother's deathbed, Hurston came to believe that her mother "looked at [her], or so [she] felt, to speak for her. She depended on [Hurston] for a voice" (63). While her detailed and repetitive returns to this scene directly reflect her commitment to telling a truth about her mother and herself, they also, in a broader sense, reflect her commitment to giving testimony to the women of her era.

Reading audiences provide a "dialogic context with authentic listener[s], which allows for a reconciliation with the broken promise, and which makes the resumption of life, in spite of the failed promise, at all possible."[43] After the failed promise, Hurston dedicated her life, through anthropology and literature, to establishing authentic listeners. The concerns that she expresses in her work stems from her desire to compensate for disappointing her mother. Speaking almost as if to her mother, she says,

> I hope Mama knows that I did my best. She must know how I have suffered for my fail-
> ure. . . . That moment was the end of a phase in my life. I was old before my time with
> grief of loss, of failure, and of remorse. No matter what the others did, my mother had
> put her trust in me. She had felt that I could and would carry out her wishes, and I had
> not. . . . I failed her. (*Dust Tracks* 64, 65)

While Hurston's testimony cannot bring her mother back to life, it performs the vital function of opening up a "dialogical process of exploration and reconciliation of two worlds—the one that was brutally destroyed and the one that is. . . . It reenacts the passage through difference in such a way, however, that it allows perhaps a certain repossession of it."[44] Hurston alludes to this very possibility of exploration and reconciliation in *Dust Tracks* when she says, "I had always thought I would be in some lone, arctic wasteland with no one under the sound of my voice. I found the cold, the desolate solitude, and earless silences, but I discovered that all that geography was in me"(83). By locating the "arctic wasteland" inside herself, Hurston maps out the terrain of a personal voyage that repeatedly takes her from the trauma of her mother's death to the act of testimony. As I suggested earlier, because the repetition of this voyage is literary, Hurston's movements between trauma and survival take on a significance that extends beyond her own individual experience.

Contrary to Robert Hemenway's view that *Dust Tracks* "fails when [Hurston] tries to shape the narrative into a statement of universality . . . suggest[ing] that the personal voyage of Zora Neale Hurston is something more than the special experience of one black woman," *Dust Tracks,* in fact, succeeds because it is the product of a repetitive process of testimonial writing. It succeeds as an exploration of the universality of the human relationship to trauma and survival. Through its thematic kinship to *Jonah's Gourd Vine* and *Their Eyes, Dust Tracks* demonstrates how the "special experience of one black woman" can empower and alter the experiences of many.[45] Out of the sorrow of failing the mother who depended on her for a voice, she shapes a career that gives voice to many. Each of Hurston's repeated returns to her mother's deathbed charts a psychic map of her life journey that corresponds to the paths of many other women, including grandmothers, mothers, and daughters.

Hurston's work establishes a frame of reference for women who reject the presence of patriarchal domination inscribed in heterosexual relations. What her works reveal about her life and the lives of her foremothers is that their social demands are so basic, so "elementary a feature of social life that its absence becomes inhuman."[46] Hurston's persistent concern with women, African American culture, and the broader American community reflects her passionate desire to disrupt a long tradition of human oppression, one she often associated with death.

CHAPTER FIVE

Hurston's Political Testimony: Trauma and Jim Crow

At the center of this project is the desire to instigate an ethically based, holistic reception of Zora Neale Hurston's work. I hope that as readers, scholars, and members of a large and diverse American culture we can better understand her efforts to dismantle a multilayered tradition of race, class, and gender oppression that relies on various levels of psychic and physical violence. My interest in her work resulted from a sense of satisfaction with Hurston's willingness to address the troubled aspects of the American social fabric that designed her era. I also felt a corresponding dissatisfaction with many of the ways that she had been critically received. Much of the criticism about Hurston's life and works focused on her use of African American dialect and her ability to use the folkloric tone and style of her Eatonville youth to examine a variety of issues. Often, the critical emphasis was not on the issues that she examines but rather on her use of language. While her use of language is worthy of praise and remains a central aspect of her work, the meaning and impetus behind it is equally important. Because Hurston's work is testimonial in nature, the ethical imperative behind her work requires that her reading audiences bear witness to her experiences and the experiences of those for whom she speaks.

Since Hurston speaks for her grandmother, her mother, and herself, her testimony includes the trauma of slavery, the intergenerational transmission of the trauma of slavery, the yoke and terrorism of Jim Crow, gender oppression, and domestic violence. During Hurston's era, scores of African American writers addressed the issues of slavery and Jim Crow, but many frame their discussions around the need to end racial discrimination and terrorism. Of course, the need was very real and urgent, and in no way do I intend to diminish the value of every effort to end racial injustice. However, there were other pressing needs as well. In recognition of these other needs, Hurston addressed the significance that lies in the way discrimination and terrorism came to an end. For Hurston, the correct way to end Jim Crow would be through white America's moral and principled compulsion to do what is humanly right. She felt that forcing hostile whites to share classrooms with black children was not only insulting, but it was potentially damaging to the self-esteem of the children.

At this point, I ask that my readers bear with me as I explain how the process of giving and receiving testimony relates to Hurston's concern with how segregation should end. In the act of testimony, those who bear witness to the speaker's trauma should, on the basis of their shared humanity, be bound in a number of ways. First, those who bear witness should receive the narrative whole and unaltered. Second, they should affirm the reality of the speaker's experience. Third, they should help the speaker to claim his or her rightful place within society. Finally, when applicable, they should acknowledge complicity and ask forgiveness for crimes committed against the individual(s) giving testimony.

Because of the traumatic history of slavery and Jim Crow, scholars and critics of African American literature can be understood as constituting a body of secondary witnesses whose interpretive role ultimately delivers the writer's testimony to the reading public, who then bears witness as well. The result of overwhelming critical emphasis on Hurston's use of language along with the corresponding silence regarding her attention to domestic violence and sociopolitical issues is that the complete process of testimony became impossible. Instead of bearing witness, her audience ignores the psychological, social, and political significance of her experiences. Refusing to be bound by any of the four processes of testimony that I mention above, many of her readers simply applauded her ability to celebrate African American culture through her use of language.

The lack of attention to the testimonial frame of her work meant that there was virtually no attention paid to Hurston's concern for the psychological health of an entire generation of African American children, who suffered the trauma of entering their classrooms under federal guard. Her rejection of legislated integration was understood as complacency toward segregation. However, Hurston publicized her vehement opposition to Jim Crow in her 1945 *Negro Digest* article, "Crazy for This Democracy"; she explains, "Jim Crow laws have been put on the books for a purpose and that purpose is psychological. . . . [T]he smallest dark child is to be convinced of its inferiority."[1] In spite of her opposition to Jim Crow, Hurston argued that integration should begin when white America felt ethically compelled to do so. The principled basis of her requirements for integration could only come about if white Americans were to place themselves in the role of secondary witnesses to the trauma of African American experiences across the nation. They would have to receive the testimonies of African Americans whole and unaltered, affirm the reality of their experiences, help African Americans to claim their rightful place in American society, and most significantly, acknowledge complicity for perpetuating the traumas of Jim Crow. Legislation took the place of this process and what America ended up with is racial tolerance that, even today, has occasion to fail.

By questioning the limits of Hurston's reception and becoming conscious of the critical tension emerging from her status as foremother of the African American literary tradition and the corresponding silence around her political views, I began to trace the stages of Hurston's testimony. The resistance to bear witness to her testimony became clear to me in 1997 during an academic conference on the interracial politics of the Harlem Renaissance. Attended by leading African American scholars, the conference featured many papers delivered on Hurston covering the usual topics. Naturally, some participants discussed her use of language and others covered the familiar territory of Hurston's role in the Harlem Renaissance. Because of the silence around the controversial aspects of Hurston's life, I decided to deliver a paper on Hurston's politics. Without detouring into the specifics of that paper, suffice it to say that my paper attempted to explain why it was perfectly reasonable for Hurston to have found *Brown vs. Board of Education,* the 1954 Supreme Court ruling for forced integration, an insult. The audience's emotional response led me to consider ways in which Hurston's works recontextualize slavery, Jim Crow, and violence against women. Understood as testimony, her works define these events as traumatic, and as such, they are more than historical anomalies remedied by legislation. Because these are traumatic events, survivors require the full process of testimony in order for any level of healing to occur.

In a broad sense, this failed testimonial process has much to do with continued racial tensions in America. This too became clear when my suggestion that Hurston's opposition to legislated integration was understandable incited an extraordinary reaction from the audience. One scholar, who had just published an article on Hurston, called her "crazy." Another, who had just published a book on her, explained that in her later years, Zora was just "bitter with disappointment." It seemed that while Hurston was named literary foremother, her title was contingent upon silence around her most controversial views. The experience helped me to develop my arguments for this project, but more significantly, it led me to bear witness to the trauma of Hurston's life and to the humanitarian project that she began as a result.

Hurston's position as trauma survivor, anthropologist, and writer shaped her attempts to instigate social change. The traumatic circumstances that framed her childhood and her adult traumas infused her testimony with cultural critiques of the historical and gender-related social conditions that made southern, rural, black women of Hurston's era vulnerable. In *Jonah's Gourd Vine, Their Eyes,* and *Dust Tracks,* Hurston's cultural critiques examine the intergenerational transmission of trauma and her own community's participation in the oppression of women. Her testimony ethically calls upon communities of southern, rural, African Americans to embrace all of their members, including women, as fully autonomous and highly valuable human beings. Hurston makes a similar call upon the Anglo American community to abandon the oppression of African Americans and all people of color. Again, her own experiences bear heavily on her testimony to the American nation as a whole. Having been southern born in 1891, Hurston experienced Jim Crow as an inevitable part of life. She expresses the personal impact of her environment in the opening lines of *Dust Tracks* by explaining that "like the dead-seeming, cold rocks, [she had] memories within that came out of the material that went to make [her]. Time and place have had their say" (1).

While Hurston claims that the all-black town of Eatonville lived peacefully alongside the white town of Maitland, there is no doubt that during her life she encountered some of the harshest forms of Jim Crow. For example, during 1938, as a member of the staff of the Federal Writers' Project, Hurston wrote an article detailing an event that had occurred in the nearby Florida town of Ocee.[2] She reports that on November 2, 1920, in the town of Ocee, only a few miles away from Eatonville, black people protested against being denied their voting rights. The white community's response was to set fire

> to a whole row of Negro houses and the wretches who had thought to hide by crawling under these buildings were shot or shot at as they fled from the flames. . . . churches had been burned. The whole Negro settlement was being assaulted. It was cried that a Negro carpenter had been beaten and castrated. . . . [The most defiant man ended up] tied to the back of a car and killed . . . his body left swinging to a telephone post beside the highway."[3]

Two months later, not far from Cross City, Florida, where Hurston would later do some of her fieldwork, the "once thriving town of Rosewood" was burned; "in early January 1920, enraged whites burned the town, killed many of its residents and drove the rest away."[4] In 1938, while doing research for the Federal Writers' Project, Hurston wrote an article entitled "Turpentine" that is the result of work-camp interviews. Her interview with a jook woman, Ethyl Robinson, uncovered "tales of beatings and forced marriages." Ethyl also shared with Hurston details about the common practice of camp supervisors to "exercise life and death control over workers." Even more alarming was the fact that "white woods riders could claim the sexual favors of any black woman in the camps. . . . If the woman's husband dared to protest, he was murdered and his body weighted with cement and thrown into the nearby Gulf of Mexico."[5]

Her encounters with Jim Crow were not limited to the South. In her 1944 article entitled "My Most Humiliating Jim Crow Experience," she describes the discrimination and humiliation she experienced during 1931 in New York while seeking medical treatment.[6] As late as 1956, four years before her death, Hurston contacted her friend, Margrit de Sahloniere, who she had not written to in a while and attributed her long silence to

> unsettling things growing out of this race disturbance here (Cocoa, FL). . . . Things began to stir unhappily in this area just about the time that your magnificent article appeared. No physical violence touched me, but the surliness, the unthinking soul of the mob prowled the state. I was too unhappy for any normal activity.[7]

These documents attest to Hurston's life-long encounters with Jim Crow in America. Her Jim Crow experiences significantly shaped her political views and added another layer to her testimonial project. This additional layer of testimony went beyond issues pertaining to Southern rural, black women and expanded upon the broader issues of nationalism and individualism.

The testimonial aspect of Hurston's work focuses on dismantling oppressive structures; therefore, much of her writing confronts the American audience's reluctant role as witness. As a result, many of her contemporaries, both black and white, were often harsh; some took steps to silence her. For example, the 1938 article "Turpentine," written for the Federal Writers' Project was, along with all of her work, "deleted from the [project's] final manuscript, which was finally published in 1993, as *The Florida Negro: A Federal Writers' Project Legacy*.[8] Similarly, large sections of her autobiography, *Dust Tracks on a Road,* were deleted at her publisher's insistence because of anti-war content. Her sarcastic comments about marines who "'consider machine guns good laxatives for heathens who get constipated with toxic ideas about a country of their own'" threatened publication.[9] While these examples illustrate how white American institutions thwarted Hurston's attempts to speak out against war and injustice, her efforts received a similar reception from certain African Americans as well.

One of the most striking examples of reluctance, on both sides of the racial line, to bear witness to Hurston's testimony against racist ideology appears in the wake of her May 1928 publication of "How It Feels to Be Colored Me." Before discussing the response, it is important to note that the thrust of the essay questions the construction of American notions of race and racialized difference.[10] Rejecting the notion of an inherent racial identity, she describes the circumstances by which external forces made her "[become] colored," and illustrates situations when she, by contrast to others, feels "most colored." At the end of the essay, she describes herself as "[t]he cosmic Zora . . . belong[ing] to no race or time, . . . [with] no separate feeling about being an American citizen and being colored . . . merely a fragment of the Great Soul that surges within the boundaries."[11] Hurston's critique of American race ideology was poorly received by two of her closest mentors during this period. Alain Locke, Hurston's mentor and black intellectual leader of the Harlem Renaissance, found Hurston's essay more alarming than anything else.

While he claims that he read it with "great pride and interest," he responded in a cautionary tone that expresses a clear lack of support for any radical expression on her part. He warns Hurston by telling her that

> maybe [she] had opened up too soon. [He] had that feeling because [he] had [him]self several times made the same mistake. The only hope is in the absolute blindness of the Caucasian mind. To the things that are really revolutionary in Negro thought and feeling they are blind.[12]

If Hurston's "only hope [was] in the blindness of the Caucasian mind," it was partly because she had little hope of support from her peers. Locke's refusal to bear witness to Hurston's testimony against an essentializing construction of racial identity is based, in part, on the success of his book, *The New Negro,* whose very title implies a racially informed identity. His 1925 edited collection had done very well and was credited with launching the Harlem Renaissance.[13] In only a few short pages, Hurston's "How It Feels to Be Colored Me," dismantles the racialized concept of being "Negro," making it inconsequential as the basis of internal identity.

Along with Locke, her benefactor was also displeased with Hurston's essay. Hurston's over-bearing white patron, Mrs. Charlotte Osgood Mason, also known as "Godmother," commanded her to explain why she wrote the article and how it came to be published. In a letter dated June 14, 1928, to Locke, Hurston avoids giving a direct explanation as to why she wrote the article.[14] In a distressed tone, she states that "Godmother didn't understand but I have explained to her now" that the article was published to "pay a debt."[15] The relationship between Hurston and her patron is too complex and distant from the subject at hand to discuss here. Suffice it to say that like the WPA editors, her publisher, and Alain Locke, Charlotte Osgood Mason was only interested in hearing very specific comments from Hurston about the racial, political, and economic conditions of American life.

In her 1950 essay, "What White Publishers Won't Print," Hurston discusses these specifics and alludes to them as a type of "colored only" script designed for black self-disclosure. The only way to get a listening audience was to tell a "story involv[ing] racial tension. It could then be offered as a study in Sociology."[16] Repeatedly chastised and rejected for attempting to throw away the "script," Hurston tried to give voice to the possibility of unracialized individualism. Her views were based on her life experiences with Jim Crow and her own upbringing in a less-than-ideal black family. As a result, she leaned toward individualism, which led her to believe that she

> did not have to consider any racial group as a whole. God made them duck by duck and that was the only way [she] could see them. [She] learned that skins were no measure of

what was inside people. So none of the Race clichés meant anything anymore. [She] began to laugh at both white and black who claimed special blessings on the basis of race.[17]

In spite of the idealistically American and potentially revolutionary basis of her request that we accept each human being as an individual, the historical time period during which Hurston lived made it politically difficult for some to accept her views.

Hurston's individualistic criteria for social acceptance opposed the general integrationist movement of her era. She lived in a historical period that emphasized integration as a response to the ongoing terrorist activity against African Americans. Between 1918 and 1932, Tuskeegee Institute reported a high incidence of lynchings, and in fact, it was not until 1952 that none were recorded at all. Using every possible resource to improve black-white relations, during the 1920s, 1930s, and 1940s the N.A.A.C.P. expected writers to be "Race" people. Literature became a political tool used according to the tenets expressed between the Harlem Renaissance left and right.

The relatively conservative right consisted of W.E.B. Du Bois, James Weldon Johnson, Jesse Fauset, and Alain Locke. On the left stood Zora Neale Hurston, Wallace Thurman, Langston Hughes, and others who tried to declare a wider range of expression for African American artists. The result was a struggle between these two groups and the white community for control of the black image. Among black writers, tensions emerged from the need to advance cultural images of fundamental similarity with the white community as a way of fostering integration while at the same underscoring distinctions that would maintain a unique cultural identity. African American artistic production during the 1920s, 1930s, and 1940s reflects this debate.

The high level of terrorism during this era placed vital importance on the effort to shape the Anglo American perception of African Americans. The increased number of lynchings and the legislation sanctioning Jim Crow attest to the significance of shaping a positive public image of African Americans. There is a direct connection between the struggle for black control of black images and the continuation of tyranny against African Americans. As Ann Douglas explains in *Terrible Honesty: Mongrel Manhattan in the 1920s,* the theatrical impetus of the New Negro stemmed from the presence of real and undeniable danger."[18] She goes on to explain that

minstrelsy was racism in action: the expropriation and distortion of black culture for white purposes and profits. . . . Johnson notes in *Black Manhattan* the "tragedy" of late-nineteenth-century black actors eager to put on *Othello* and *Hamlet* but forced to make a living by doing darky routines that whites expected and applauded.[19]

While the artistic expressions of the Harlem Renaissance reflect the collaboration of both blacks and whites, the struggle over how those expressions become public images of blackness remained a contested issue.

Hurston's anthropological training led her to celebrate the retention of Africanisms in black American culture and to document the distinct forms of cultural production that emerge through folklore, music, and religion.[20] Like others during her era, she recognized that because of the proximity to each other and the effects of hybridity, Americans (black and white) are products of a cultural exchange that, ultimately, produces American popular culture.

In her 1934 essay, "Characteristics of Negro Expression," Hurston identifies this process of exchange in her discussion of black and white musical expression:

> Everyone is familiar with the Negro's modification of the whites' musical instruments, so that his interpretation has been adopted by the white man himself and then reinterpreted. In so many words, Paul Whiteman is giving an imitation of a Negro orchestra making use of white-invented musical instruments in a Negro way. Thus has arisen a new art in the civilized world, and thus has our so-called civilization come.[21]

Attempting to acknowledge the exchange between blacks and whites that constitute American culture, Hurston refused to create representations of essentialized blackness struggling against the forces of white oppression. This refusal was seen as a contradiction to the sociopolitical efforts of many of her peers, and some retaliated. For example, in his June 1, 1938, review of *Their Eyes* in *Opportunity,* Alain Locke attacks Hurston for not "com[ing] to grips with motive fiction and social document fiction."[22] Similarly, in his October 5, 1937, review of *Their Eyes* in the *New Masses,* Richard Wright accuses Hurston of

> *voluntarily* continu[ing] in her novel the tradition, which was *forced* upon the Negro in the theater, that is, the minstrel technique that makes the "white folks" laugh. Her characters eat and laugh and cry and work and kill; they swing like a pendulum eternally in that safe and narrow orbit in which America likes to see the Negro live, between laughter and tears.[23]

Both Wright and Locke make Hurston's crime quite clear: Her characters dared to reflect the full range of human living. In doing so, they went beyond classifications of constructed racial identities and beyond the perimeters of the designated political struggle.

Ironically, Hurston's approach to African American culture is extremely political in nature. By not representing the African American effort to move beyond oppressive and restrictive social strata, Hurston's work attempts to sabotage the American system of social stratification that relies on the authority of racial, economic, and gendered classifications. Hurston explains the basis of her views quite clearly by stating that she has been a Negro three times—a Negro baby, a Negro girl and a Negro woman. Still, if you have no clear-cut impression of what the Negro in America is like, then you are in the same place with [her]. There is no *The Negro* here. Our lives are so diversified, internal attitudes so varied, appearances and capabilities so different, that there is no possible classification so catholic that it will cover us all, except My people! My people![24]

As I discussed earlier, critics continue to struggle with Hurston's political views and remain puzzled by her attempt to place an ethical prerequisite on integration. When her work reflects radical gestures that demand America give all that they morally owe, she is often referred to as "crazy" or "bitter." Even her most direct literary descendent, Alice Walker, describes Zora in her later life as "frightened . . . and her work reactionary, static, shockingly misguided, and timid."[25] Readers seem most comfortable with her work when they limit their focus to those particular aspects of her texts that reflect their own agendas. As a result, whether referring to Robert Hemenway's assertion that Zora Neale Hurston "remained committed to her work [and] the honest portraiture of her race," or to Cheryl Wall's claim that "Hurston's respect for the cultural traditions of black people is the most important constant in her career," or to almost any one of the numerous scholarly texts, articles, and essays that critique her works, one will find that the vast majority concur that Hurston's central concern was to impress upon America the value of African American culture.[26] In fact, Hurston was also very concerned with impressing upon America the value of mirroring American democratic ideology in democratic practice by granting all citizens access to voting booths, schools, and other public venues. While she experienced a sense of incongruence in her life resulting from personal trauma, this was intensified by the incongruence of her status as an American citizen living under Jim Crow laws. The reluctance to critically evaluate the effects of trauma on Hurston's life, including Jim Crow, has severely limited our understanding of her.

When, for example, Walker describes Hurston's later work as "reactionary, static, shockingly misguided and timid," Walker fails to take into account the long-term effects of Hurston's failure to locate, among the American reading public, secondary witnesses—those who would receive her testimony.[27] Hurston's first two novels, *Jonah's Gourd Vine* and *Their Eyes Were Watching God,* and her autobiography, *Dust Tracks on a Road,* are each increments of a testimony to the shattering events of her personal life, which are complicated by living in a Jim Crow society that uses constructions of race, class, and gender ideologies as tools to traumatize. In her address of these broader, sociopolitical concerns, some of Hurston's other works can be understood as culturally testimonial.

For example, her third novel, *Moses, Man of the Mountain* (1939), recasts the biblical figure of Moses and the story of the exodus using African American dialect and folk traditions. By recasting the book of Exodus, Hurston addresses the psychological difficulties of leading a people out of a slave mentality. The novel does not accentuate the pragmatic difficulties of the journey to independence. Instead, Hurston focuses broadly on intergenerational trauma, which she dealt with on an intimate level in her first novel, *Jonah's Gourd Vine* (1934). In this text, Moses finds it difficult to lead because his people have had hundreds of years of fear beaten into them. The violent trauma of their history has made them afraid. Every obstacle makes them want to "go back to Egypt where [they think they] belong" (314). Hurston presents their cowardly reaction to fighting for their own place in the world as indicative of this particular generation's close proximity to slavery. They react as slaves because they have been conditioned to do nothing else. Through this novel, Hurston calls for an end to slavery's legacy of fear by first pointing out the impossibility of designing a new "free" state with "slave" ideals. Like the biblical leader, she solves the problem by having Moses proclaim that "none of [the] slave-minded cowards will enter the land [God] promised them. They shall wander in this wilderness until they are dead" (315). Hurston identifies the obstacle that prohibits entry into a free state as a fear-filled slave mentality that evolves out of violent, traumatic conditions.

Her focus on the cultural and psychological response to the trauma of slavery places this novel within the thematic category of trauma narrative. Like her first two novels, *Moses, Man of the Mountain* expresses her concern with the communities formed by trauma survivors. Most specifically, as addressed in *Moses, Man of the Mountain,* she is concerned that the repetition associated with trauma does not adversely affect subsequent generations. By shifting focus away from an analysis of the racist conditions of Jim Crow, and, instead, identifying the central problem of the masses as an internalization of the trauma of slavery, Hurston addresses the crippling effects of intergenerational trauma. As I discussed in chapter 1, intergenerational trauma is "passed down as the family legacy even to children born after the trauma. . . . Different cultures capitalize on different pathways to acculturate their young. Thus, beyond the familial, from parents to offspring, entire bodies of human endeavor are vehicles of transmission."[28] Through *Moses, Man of the Mountain,* Hurston expresses her desire that the future of African American life be informed by free-minded (versus slave-minded) individuals and ideologies. This would minimize the transmission of fear-based survival forms that worked well in slavery but fail to provide a basis for building a free and equal state of existence.

Her solution was to look toward the next generation. Hurston was quite concerned with the future of black children. She wrote letters calling for an improvement in children's education to the Florida Board of Education, and her essay, "The Rise of the Begging Joints" (1944), demands that educational leaders raise the standard of black education. In *Moses, Man of the Mountain,* she expresses her hope that children will manifest a liberated sense of their own identity; Moses says, "'I can make something out of their children but not of them. . . .' [The] next day Moses turned the hosts of Israel back into the wilderness to serve their forty years and grow men and women in place of slaves" (316). She ends the chapter with a hopeful edict from God: "'The third generation will feel free and noble. Then I can mold a nation'" (317). Hurston's novel addresses the potentially crippling effects of intergenerational trauma by calling attention to its repetitive patterns and exploring ways of stopping the perpetuation of psychological slavery.

Hurston makes clear her desire for internal freedom at the end of *Moses, Man of the Mountain*, when she makes her readers privy to one of Moses' reflective moments. Here, Hurston links the need to reduce the impact of intergenerational trauma to her faith in individual effort. Moses' ultimate discovery is that "no man may make another free. Freedom was something internal. The outside signs were just signs and symbols of the man inside. All you could do was to give the opportunity for freedom and the man himself must make his own emancipation" (344, 345). Emancipation, for Hurston, is tied as much to the psychological state of African Americans as it is to the repeal of Jim Crow laws. Her textual emphasis on testimony and healing demonstrates her conviction that both types of emancipation are necessary. Without the internal liberation from the repetitive bonds of trauma, repeal of Jim Crow laws means little; human beings are easily enslaved by their histories.

Hurston's last novel, *Seraph on the Suwanee* (1948), continues her traumatic testimony by returning to her concern with female emancipation. The novel has long been regarded as problematic. Alice Walker, for example, holds *Seraph* up as evidence of Hurston's late-life misguidedness because it is a novel about white people for whom, she says, no one cares."[29] The story develops around the love affair between Jim and Arvay and revisits the same issues that Hurston raises in *Jonah's Gourd Vine* and *Their Eyes*—patriarchal control of women. The connection between these novels and *Seraph* is only evident by tracing the narrative reappearance of traumatic sites in Hurston's life.

In *Seraph on the Suwanee* Hurston revisits the scene of her mother's death, particularly the conversation she describes in *Jonah's Gourd Vine* and *Dust Tracks* when Lucy asks her daughter to ensure that folk ritual would not be carried out as she died. Lucy did not want her mirror covered, her bed turned east, or her pillow removed. In *Seraph*, Arvay fulfills her mother's deathbed wish by burying her the way she wants. Arvay's response to her mother's deathbed wish that she can "put her dying dependence" in her redeems Hurston's own failure as a child (280). In *Dust Tracks* Hurston recalls that her dying mother "put her trust in me. She felt that I could and would carry out her wishes, and I had not" (64). The writing of *Seraph* allows Hurston to revise a portion of her testimony to the trauma of her mother's death. She revises the portion that had caused her the most guilt, and in doing so, attempts to fictionally honor her mother's wishes.

The other recurring testimonial theme that Hurston revises in *Seraph* is the complexity of heterosexual gender relations. In this novel, Hurston renders the total submission that Jim requires of Arvay, and this is in stark contrast with Janie in *Their Eyes* who kills her rabid lover in favor of her own independent life. As Claudia Tate observes, Janie "signifies freedom and possibility beyond the novel's close," whereas at the ending of *Seraph* "all desire is consummated, Arvay and Jim are symbolically dead."[30] Through Jim and Arvay's relationship, Hurston continues her critique of patriarchal romantic love. Hurston's creation of a white woman character who "was serving and was meant to serve" should be contrasted with her black female character, Janie, who, ultimately, serves the needs of her own inner quest.

The polarized endings of the two love stories reveal Hurston's continued concern about the domination of women. The depiction of a frail, blond, white woman (the romantic ideal) as willing to submit to male domination in the name of love allows Hurston to critique the price that women pay for being highly valued as frail, white, and blond. Her critique is meant for the benefit of black and white women alike, who are both objectified as sexual objects that must be controlled.

Her shift from black to white characters to discuss patriarchal domination underscores the ways in which gender and race constructions are used to alter the very basis of human identity. For example, in her earlier novel, *Their Eyes,* the varying degrees of a woman's blackness indicate the required amount of effort needed to dominate her. Tea Cake did not have to slap light-skinned Janie very hard because her bruises would easily show. The other men in town complained that it was difficult to bruise their darker-skinned women and so they had to be ready to fight harder and longer to demonstrate their power over the women. In Hurston's last novel, *Seraph,* Arvay physically embodies the male-defined American ideal of blond beauty. Arvay's willing submission to her man is the result of her acceptance of a patriarchally ordered gender role that defines her womanhood through servitude and silence (308, 311).

While *Seraph on the Suwanee* is Hurston's last novel, she does not abandon her project of testimony or her concern for women. After its publication in 1948, her longest work comprises a series of articles for the *Pittsburgh Courier* from 1952 to 1953 reporting on the trial of Ruby McCollum. McCollum was the black mistress of a white doctor and state senator, Leroy Adams. He had fathered one of her children, and she was pregnant again when she shot him during an argument. During a notoriously unfair trial, she was convicted of first-degree murder. Hurston and the *Courier* became very active in defending McCollum because they believed that her right to a fair trial had been violated on the basis of race and gender. Hurston's interest in McCollum demonstrates her continued concern for women's relative powerlessness in American society.

After looking at the traumas of Hurston's personal life and contextualizing these events socially and politically just as she did, it becomes clear that the general movement of her work expands from an intimately personal testimony outward toward a broader cultural and political testimony. Hurston never abandons her concern for the psychological health of women, children, and Americans in general. Her testimonial project begins close to home as she examines her mother's life through the female protagonist's relative powerlessness in *Jonah's Gourd Vine.* The intimacy of her testimony continues as she gives testimony to her own struggle with violence through *Their Eyes.* Her next novel, *Moses, Man of the Mountain,* examines intergenerational trauma, but the social context moves beyond Hurston's individual self to address the psychological health of the broader African American community. In *Dust Tracks* she takes a backward glance at her own development, revisits the site of her own trauma, and out of this, provides a humanitarian discussion of American race relations. Her final novel, *Seraph on the Suwanee,* moves beyond her own black community to offer a critique of the ways that patriarchal domination works against poor white women as well.

By considering her emphasis on the psychological health of American communities, it is understandable that in 1954, at the age of 63 and after a lifetime of Jim Crow, Hurston rejected *forced* integration in favor of a consensual one. It is equally understandable that in 1945, at the age of 54, she would publicly offer "[her] hand, [her] heart and [her] head to the total struggle. [She] is for the complete repeal of all Jim Crow laws in the United States once and for all. For the benefit of this nation and as a precedent to the world."[31]

Similarly, in the same year she publishes "Crazy for This Democracy" and sarcastically promises that if she ever comes across a true "sample of [democracy she] sure will try it. [She] [doesn't] know for [her]self, but [she] [has] been told that it is really wonderful." She goes on to point out that with all the grand talk about democracy no one has mentioned that Jim Crow rule dominates South Africa, East India, all of colonial Africa, Asia, the Netherlands, and the East Indies: "The Arse-and All of Democracy has shouldered the load of subjugating the dark world completely."[32]

Perhaps when Walker described Hurston's later life as misguided, what she was alluding to was the 1955 letter to the *Orlando Sentinel,* "Court Order Can't Make Races Mix." Hurston wrote this letter in response to the May 17, 1954, Supreme Court order to force school integration. The court order symbolized a great accomplishment for those who had dedicated their lives to destroying the separate but equal policies that supported Jim Crow. However, Hurston offered an alternate view that is equally legitimate and powerful. Life in the South and under the rule of Jim Crow educated Hurston enough to know that black children were not welcomed in white schools. She was all too familiar with the violence and degradation associated with attempts to integrate the South. Within the context of her experiences, her concern for the psychological health of her community's children caused her to reject forced integration. Her own self-sufficiency and faith in African American culture led her to explain how "the Supreme Court would have pleased [her] more if they had concerned themselves with enforcing the compulsory education provisions for Negroes in the South as it is done for white children. . . . Growth from within. Ethical and cultural desegregation."[33] In essence, Hurston asks for racial justice compelled by ethical principles, not law.

A similar set of ethics should compel students and scholars of Hurston's life and work to examine even the most controversial aspects of her life. Because Hurston is the African American literary foremother, her joyous, celebratory, boundary-breaking fiction should be holistically contextualized along with her political views. The complexity of Hurston's character is apparent when one contrasts her willingness to participate in a violent protest of Jim Crow with her deep despair over World War II. In 1944, she wrote a long-time friend and colleague expressing the burden she felt in a world where the

> enormous pest of hate [is] rotting men's souls. When will people learn that you cannot quarantine hate? Once it gets loose in the world, it rides over all barriers and seeps under the doors and in the cracks of every house. I see it all around me every day. I am not just talking of race hatred. Just hate. Everybody is at it. Kill, rend and tear! Women who are supposed to be the softening influence in life screaming for the kill. Once it was just Germany and Japan and Italy. Now, it is our allies as well. . . . The world smells like an abattoir. It makes me very unhappy. I am all wrong in this vengeful world. I will to love.[34]

Hurston's deep-felt passion and the historical climate of her era fostered extreme reactions that refused participation in essentializing discourse. Instead, she focused on how segregation, colonialism, and domestic violence dehumanized Americans. Because she is a trauma survivor, she continually returns to exploring definitions of *human* identity.

This reading of Hurston's works offers an alternative perspective on the centrality of race, gender, and class identities. A similar reading of other African American texts that are considered central to the formation of the African American literary canon will further resituate our understanding of constructed identities and provide a space for theoretical exploration on the basis of individual human identity. The texts that immediately come to mind are Frederick Douglass's *Narrative of the Life of Frederick Douglass* (1845), W.E.B. Du Bois's *Souls of Black Folk* (1903), Booker T. Washington's *Up from Slavery* (1901), Harriet Jacobs's *Incidents in the Life of a Slave Girl* (1861), Harriet Wilson's *Our Nig* (1859) and Richard Wright's *Black Boy* (1945). There are many, many others that would benefit from such a reading as well. Because these texts are organized around the development of racialized identities within a racially hostile society, reading them as traumatic testimony will displace what we have come to understand as the main mechanisms of social stratification—constructions of race, class, and gender. Reading these works through the lens of trauma theory will allow us to re-evaluate the wide range of artistic production that inherently transgresses the boundaries of race, class, gender, and historicity. If we understand the proliferation of poetry, prose, drama, jazz, blues, and dance as reproductive acts that attempt to locate a raceless, genderless, classless, and timeless essence of human identity, we can begin to explore the range of potential healing that rests in these forms of testimony.

Rereading these texts as trauma testimony has the potential to accomplish two important goals. First, it can demonstrate the extent to which race, class, and gender identity constructions serve as psychological weapons for alienating and dehumanizing others. Second, it can illustrate how artistic production creates alternate communities of secondary witnesses and simultaneously constructs the basis for alternate identities. The value of using our understanding of trauma testimony to reread the African American canon rests in the potential healing for a large population of young people who, because they are members of marginalized groups, feel vulnerable or degraded by virtue of their race, class, or gender position. As a result, they often engage in self-destructive patterns of behavior. A psychoanalytic reading of African American literature has the potential to reveal the *process* of internal oppression and emancipation, sorrow and celebration. It has the potential to unveil the psychological process of human survival in the wake of trauma.

Notes

Introduction

1. Pamela Bordelon, ed., *Go Gator and Muddy the Water: Writings by Zora Neale Hurston from the Federal Writers' Project* (New York: W. W. Norton, 1999) 3, 5.
2. Dori Laub, "Bearing Witness or the Vicissitudes of Listening," *Testimony: Crisis of Witnessing in Literature, Psychoanalysis, and History,* Shoshana Felman and Dori Laub (New York: Routledge, 1992) 5.
3. Elizabeth Pleck, *Domestic Tyranny: The Making of American Social Policy Against Family Violence from Colonial Times to the Present* (New York: Oxford UP, 1987) 182.
4. For further reading on race and class issues in the feminists' movements of the 1960s and 1970s, see bell hooks's essay "Black Women: Shaping Feminist Theory," *Feminist Theory: From Margin to Center* (Boston: South End Press, 1984).
5. The following are two examples of varied attempts to contextualize the violence in *Their Eyes Were Watching God:* In 1985, Marks notes that the violence in *Their Eyes* signals Hurston's inability to explain the phenomenon of domestic violence: "Janie, as well as Hurston, is unable to come to terms with the violence Hurston finds inherent in heterosexual relationships." Donald Marks, "Sex, Violence, and Organic Consciousness in Zora Neale Hurston's *Their Eyes Were Watching God,*" *Black American Literature Forum,* 19 (1985): 152–157. Offering a sociopolitical reading of the violence in *Their Eyes,* Cheryl Wall finds that even though "no voice in the text rises to condemn Tea Cake's violence . . . the scene's configuration makes the connection between that violence and the capitalist, racist, and elitist values [represented by specific characters];" see Cheryl Wall, *Women of the Harlem Renaissance* (Bloomington: Indiana UP, 1993) 190.
6. Beth E. Richie, "Battered Black Women: A Challenge for the Black Community," *Words of Fire: An Anthology of African American Feminist Thought,* ed. Beverly Guy-Sheftall (New York: New York UP, 1995) 399–400. During her research, Richie contacted a group called "Battered Minority Women" (BMW) and found them articulating a belief that demanded silence as her initial response to violence against black women. BMW explained, "black women are beaten solely because their men are deprived. . . . Black women should involve themselves in the struggle for racial justice in order to end battering in their own homes . . . responsibility lies with white society." In addition, the silence around domestic violence in the black community has a sociopolitical context that is connected to the racial uplift movements of the late nineteenth and early twentieth centuries. For an informative discussion, I suggest Kevin K. Gaines's *Uplifting*

the Race: Black Leadership, Politics and Culture in the Twentieth Century (Chapel Hill: North Carolina UP, 1996). Gaines argues that while uplift ideology is a broad term with a debatable definition, one of the dominant approaches to racial uplift restricted women; he explains, "gender conflict exposed the contradictions of uplift's vision of progress, a middle class vision structured in sexual dominance" (136).

7. Richie, "Battered Black Women: A Challenge for the Black Community," 399.

8. Gaines, *Uplifting the Race: Black Leadership, Politics and Culture in the Twentieth Century* (Chapel Hill: North Carolina UP, 1996). For an informative discussion of the development and impact of African American uplift ideologies, I suggest a full reading Gaines's text.

9. Freud's work on trauma is a continuation of the work begun by Pierre Janet and Jean Martin Charcot. Janet distinguished between traumatic memory and narrative memory, arguing that traumatic memory has no social component, and narrative memory does. He also established the notion of the subconscious, fixed ideas that influence perceptions and behaviors. Freud would later develop upon Janet's notion of the subconscious to discuss hysteria and dissociation. This work became the foundation for trauma studies. For an informative discussion, see Bessel A. Van Der Kolk and Onno Van Der Hart, "The Intrusive Past: The Flexibility of Memory and the Engraving of Trauma," *Trauma: Explorations in Memory,* ed. Cathy Caruth (Baltimore: Johns Hopkins UP, 1995). Also see, Josef Breuer and Sigmund Freud, *Studies on Hysteria,* Trans. James Strachey (1895. New York: Basic Books, 1999).

10. Sigmund Freud, *Beyond the Pleasure Principle* (1893; New York: W.W. Norton, 1989) 11.

11. Freud, *Beyond,* 11.

12. Freud, *Beyond,* 15.

13. Freud, *Beyond,* 16.

14. Freud, *Beyond,* 17.

15. Freud, *Beyond,* 17.

16. Geoffrey Hartman, "Shoah and the Intellectual Witness," *Partisan Review* 1 (1998): 37. I use the term "secondary witness" (coined by des Pres and Langer) interchangeably with Hartman's "intellectual witness." He defines this witness as engaging in "active reception that is relevant both for our time and the encroaching future . . . [addressing] with similar force a community and the public. [He looks] . . . at the possibility of intellectual witness[ing] [among] those who did not directly experience the Nazi era as well as in survivors whose writings are extant and exemplary."

17. Alvin Rosenfeld, "Jean Améry as Witness," *Holocaust Remembrance: The Shapes of Memory,* ed. Geoffrey Hartman (Cambridge: Blackwell, 1994) 60. Rosenfeld examines the role of readers of testimony in relation to the act of writing by Holocaust victims who, even as they wrote, knew they probably would not survive. He uses the works of Holocaust victim Jean Améry to link the role of the testifier to the role of the listener.

18. Rosenfeld, "Jean Améry as Witness," *Holocaust Remembrance: The Shapes of Memory,* ed. Geoffrey Hartman, 66.

19. Esther Rashkin, *Family Secrets and the Psychoanalysis of Narrative* (Princeton: Princeton UP, 1992) 4–5. Rashkin analyzes narratives that are "organized by the inscription within them of a particular kind of secret" (4). She reads these organizing inscriptions in the works of Joseph Conrad, Auguste de Villiers de l'Isle-Adam, Henry James, Edgar Allan Poe, and Honoré de Balzac. Cathy Caruth's *Unclaimed Experience: Trauma, Narrative, and History* traces the study of trauma testimony in literature to Freud's description of traumatic experience in his analysis of Tasso's epic *Gerusalemme Liberata.* She defines this act as appropriate since "literature, like psychoanalysis, is interested in the complex relation between knowing and not knowing. And it is . . . at the specific point at which knowing and not knowing intersect that the language of

literature and the psychoanalytic theory of traumatic experience precisely meet" (3). Using Hurston as a model, this project seeks to resituate the psychological effects of race, class, and gender constructions on inscriptions of trauma and silence.

20. K. J. Phillips, "The Phalaris Syndrome: Alain Robbe-Grillet vs. D. M. Thomas," *Women and Violence in Literature: An Essay Collection,* ed. Katherine Anne Ackley (New York: Garland Publishing, 1990) 176, 180.

21. Cathy Caruth, *Unclaimed Experience: Trauma, Narrative, and History* (Baltimore: Johns Hopkins UP, 1996) 2.

22. Suzette A. Henke, *Trauma and Testimony in Women's Life Writing* (New York: St. Martin's, 2000). In this second edition, Henke offers an insightful analysis of the testimonial nature of the works of Colette, Hilda Doolittle, Anais Nin, Janet Frame, Audre Lord, and Sylvia Fraser.

23. Cathy Caruth, *Unclaimed Experience: Trauma, Narrative, and History* (Baltimore: Johns Hopkins UP, 1996) 8.

24. Laura S. Brown, "Not outside the Range," *Trauma: Explorations in Memory* ed. Cathy Caruth (Baltimore: Johns Hopkins UP, 1995) 102.

25. Brown, "Not outside the Range," 102, 107.

26. Lawrence Langer, *Holocaust Testimonies: The Ruins of Memory* (New Haven: Yale UP, 1991) xv.

27. Amy S. Gottfried, *Historical Nightmares and Imaginative Violence in American Women's Writings* (Westwood: Greenwood Press, 1998) 9.

28. Joel Williamson, *The Crucible of Race: Black-White Relations in the American South Since Emancipation* (New York: Oxford UP, 1984) 111. During Hurston's era, testimony and silence within the African American community reflected the need to dispel the postreconstruction propaganda that publicly depicted the essential nature of African Americans as "bestial, and [argued] that, unsupported by the enforced moral behavior of slavery, the New Negro was reverting to native savagery." African American attempts to dispel this notion of the savage black male roaming the countryside in search of white women to beat and rape demanded silence concerning any discussion of domestic violence within the African American community. Part of the campaign for equality required the image of a flawless African American community, morally sound, intellectually competent, and, above all, harmless.

29. James A. Snead, "Repetition as a Figure of Black Culture," *Black Literature and Literary Theory,* ed. Henry Louis Gates (New York: Routledge, 1990) 75. Snead addresses the long process of healing by identifying the "outstanding fact of the late twentieth-century [as] its ongoing reconciliation with black culture. The mystery may be that it took so long to discern the elements of black culture already there in latent form, and to realize that the separation between the cultures was perhaps all along not one of nature, but one of force."

30. Shoshana Felman, "Education and Crisis, Or the Vicissitudes of Teaching," *Testimony: Crisis of Witnessing in Literature, Psychoanalysis, and History,* Shoshana Felman and Dori Laub, M.D. (New York: Routledge, 1992) 5.

31. Kali Tal, *Worlds of Hurt: Reading the Literatures of Trauma* (Cambridge: Cambridge UP, 1996) 17.

32. While short stories such as "Sweat"(1926) and "Spunk"(1925) reflect the power dynamics and potential violence of heterosexual relations that concerned Hurston, they are not lengthy enough to fully contextualize her personal relationship to this issue.

33. David Levering Lewis, *When Harlem Was in Vogue* (New York: Oxford UP, 1981) 95, 97. *Opportunity Magazine* was an organ of the Urban League. It was launched in January 1923, with Charles Johnson as its editor. By September, Johnson began awarding prizes for outstanding creative achievement. Johnson wrote that his aim was "'to encourage the reading of literature both by Negro authors and about Negro life, not merely because they are Negro authors but because what they write is literature.'"

34. Larry Neal, Introduction, *Jonah's Gourd Vine* by Zora Neale Hurston (New York: Lippincott, 1972) 1–9.
35. Cheryl Wall, "Changing Her Own Words," *Zora Neale Hurston: Critical Perspectives Past and Present,* eds. Henry Louis Gates and K.A. Appiah (New York: Amistad Press, 1993) 77.
36. Zora Neale Hurston, "Characteristics of Negro Expression," *Zora Neale Hurston: Folklore Memoirs and Other Writings,* ed. Cheryl Wall (New York: Library of America, 1995) 838.
37. Geoffrey Hartman, *Holocaust Remembrance: The Shapes of Memory* (Cambridge: Blackwell, 1994) 19.
38. Henry Louis Gates, *"Race," Writing, and Difference* (Chicago: University of Chicago Press, 1985) 11.
39. Henry Louis Gates, Preface, *The Classic Slave Narratives* (New York: Penguin, 1987) xiii.
40. Claudia Tate, *Psychoanalysis and Black Novels: Desire and the Protocols of Race* (New York: Oxford UP, 1998) 179.
41. Ralph Ellison, rev. of *Their Eyes Were Watching God,* by Zora Neale Hurston, *New Masses* May 1941: 211.
42. H.R. Brock rev. of *Jonah's Gourd Vine,* by Zora Neale Hurston, *New York Times Book Review* November 10, 1935: 4.
43. Claudia Tate, *Psychoanalysis and Black Novels: Desire and the Protocols of Race* (New York: Oxford UP, 1998) 181.
44. Hazel Carby, "The Politics of Fiction, Anthropology, and the Folk: Zora Neale Hurston," *History and Memory in African American Culture,* eds. Geneviève Fabre and Robert O'Meally (New York: Oxford UP, 1994) 35.
45. Saul Friedländer, "Trauma, Memory, and Transference," *Holocaust Remembrance: The Shapes of Memory,* ed. Geoffrey Hartman (Cambridge: Blackwell, 1994) 261.
46. Zora Neale Hurston, "How it Feels to Be Colored Me," *Zora Neale Hurston: Folklore Memoirs and Other Writings,* ed. Cheryl Wall (New York: Library of America, 1995) 826.
47. Robert Hemenway, *Zora Neale Hurston: A Literary Biography* (Urbana: U of Illinois P, 1977) 39, 22. For further reading on Hurston and the Harlem Renaissance, I suggest Cheryl Wall's text, *Women of the Harlem Renaissance.* In addition, David Levering Lewis's text, *When Harlem Was in Vogue,* provides a good overview of Hurston's relationship to this movement.

Chapter 1: Intergenerational Trauma in *Jonah's Gourd Vine*

1. Sigmund Freud, *Beyond the Pleasure Principle* (1893; New York: W.W. Norton 1989) 12.
2. Robert Hemenway, *Zora Neale Hurston: A Literary Biography* (Urbana: U of Illinois P, 1977) 189. Hemenway explains that Hurston had no income while she wrote and "[b]y the time the manuscript was completed, she owed eighteen dollars in rent, and on the morning of October 16th the landlord evicted her."
3. John Chamberlain, rev. of *Jonah's Gourd Vine,* by Zora Neale Hurston, *The New York Times* May 3, 1934: 7.
4. David Levering Lewis, *When Harlem Was in Vogue* (New York: Knopf, 1981) 91.
5. Hemenway, *Zora Neale Hurston: A Literary Biography,* 189.
6. Hemenway, *Zora Neale Hurston: A Literary Biography,* 189.
7. Hemenway, *Zora Neale Hurston: A Literary Biography,* 190.
8. Hemenway, *Zora Neale Hurston: A Literary Biography,* 14, 15, 189.
9. Hemenway, *Zora Neale Hurston: A Literary Biography,* 16.
10. Hemenway, *Zora Neale Hurston: A Literary Biography,* 15.

11. Kevin Gaines, *Uplifting the Race: Black Leadership, Politics, and Culture in the Twentieth Century* (Chapel Hill: U of North Carolina P, 1996) 5.

12. Gaines, Uplifting the Race: Black Leadership, Politics, and Culture in the Twentieth Century, 5.

13. Zora Neale Hurston, *Dust Tracks on a Road* (Philadelphia: J. P. Lippincott, 1942) 251.

14. I allude to Joseph Campbell's *Hero with a Thousand Faces* (Princeton: Princeton UP, 1949), which traces the archetypal patterns of quest heroes as they appear in a variety of cultures from antiquity to the twentieth century.

15. Zora Neale Hurston, *Jonah's Gourd Vine,* 4, 5, 6. The year 1881 is based on the information given in the conversation between Ned and Amy Crittenden. John's mother, Amy Crittenden, "wuz twelve years old when Lee made de big surrender." Ned states that John is sixteen years old and that she had him when they got married and they have been married for twelve years.

16. Franz Fanon, *Black Skin, White Masks* (New York: Grove Press, 1967) 192. I define this term, "postbellum neurosis," based on Fanon's analysis of the black Antillean. The similarities between the black Antillean who lives "an ambiguity that is extraordinarily neurotic" and Hurston's characterization of Ned are striking. Fanon explains that the "Antillean has recognized himself as a Negro, but, by virtue of an ethical transit, he also feels (collective unconscious) that one is a Negro to the degree to which one is wicked, sloppy, malicious, instinctual. Everything that is opposite of these Negro modes of behavior is white. . . . In other words, he who is Negro is immoral. If I order my life like that of a moral man, I am simply not a Negro"; here, Fanon provides a psychological explanation of Ned's worldview as well.

17. Franz Fanon, *Black Skin, White Masks,* 192.

18. Robert O'Meally and Geneviève Fabre, *History and Memory in African-American Culture* (Oxford: Oxford UP, 1994) 6.

19. Franz Fanon, *Black Skin, White Masks,* 10–11.

20. I use the term "African American history" to refer to the unique experiences of black people in America but not to imply that Anglo American history is separate; the two histories are interdependent.

21. Winthrop Jordan, *The White Man's Burden: Historical Origins of Racism in the United States* (London: Oxford, UP, 1974) 126.

22. Edmund S. Morgan, *American Slavery: American Freedom* (New York, W.W. Norton & Company, 1975) 312. The 1669 Virginia legislation serves as an example of the type of laws that appeared in many slave-holding states. It guaranteed the slave-owner immunity from prosecution if he happened, by chance, to kill a resisting slave. The rational was that only by accident would anyone "destroy his own estate."

23. Frederick Douglass, *Narrative of the Life of Frederick Douglass, an American Slave* (New York: W.W. Norton, 1997) 68.

24. Morgan, *American Slavery: American Freedom,* 313.

25. Joel Williamson, *The Crucible of Race* (New York: Oxford UP, 1984) 44.

26. This paragraph relies on information from Herbert Aptheker's *A Documentary History of the Negro People in the United States* (New York: First Carol Press, 1990).

27. Williamson, *The Crucible of Race,* 226. "Reconstruction had definitely died in the lower South [by] 1877."

28. Williamson, *The Crucible of Race,* 79.

29. W.E.B. Du Bois, *Souls of Black Folk* (1903; New York: First Vintage, 1990) 130.

30. Williamson, *The Crucible of Race,* 57.

31. Du Bois, *Souls of Black Folk* (1903; New York: First Vintage, 1990) 34.

32. Williamson, *The Crucible of Race,* 224.

33. Cathy Caruth, *Unclaimed Experience: Trauma, Narrative, and History* (Baltimore: Johns Hopkins UP, 1996) 3.

34. Caruth, *Unclaimed Experience: Trauma, Narrative, and History,* 5.

35. Caruth, *Unclaimed Experience: Trauma, Narrative, and History,* 5.

36. Shoshana Felman, Introduction, *Testimony: Crisis of Witnessing in Literature, Psychoanalysis, and History,* Shoshana Felman and Dori Laub (New York: Routledge, 1992) 5.

37. Caruth, *Unclaimed Experience: Trauma, Narrative, and History,* 3.

38. Caruth, *Unclaimed Experience: Trauma, Narrative, and History,* 57–58, 131. Currently, there are two dominant trends in the study of trauma. The first focuses on "trauma as the 'shattering' of a previously whole self," and the second focuses on "the survival function of trauma as allowing one to get through an overwhelming experience by numbing oneself to it."

39. Du Bois, *Souls of Black Folk,* 8.

40. Fanon, *Black Skin, White Masks,* 142, 143, 145.

41. Yael Danieli, ed. *International Handbook of Multigenerational Legacies of Trauma* (New York: Plenum Press, 1998) 9.

42. Yael Danieli, ed. *International Handbook of Multigenerational Legacies of Trauma,* 10.

43. I refer to studies of the Holocaust made by scholars born after the event. For further reading on the ethical duty to reconstitute the past of survivors with whom one has a literal, national, or religious kinship and the attempt to do so out of stories rather than experience, see Norma Rosen's "The Second Life of Holocaust Imagery" in *Accidents of Influence: Writing as Woman and a Jew in America.* Also, see *Holocaust Remembrance: the Shapes of Memory,* ed. Geoffrey H. Hartman.

44. William E. Cross, "Black Psychological Functioning and the Legacy of Slavery: Myths and Realities," *International Handbook of Multigenerational Legacies of Trauma,* ed. Yael Danieli (New York: Plenum Press, 1998) 387.

45. Zora Neale Hurston, *Jonah's Gourd Vine,* 203. Hurston's glossary defines patter rollers as "[p]atrollers, an organization of the late slavery days that continued through the reconstruction period. Its main objective was the intimidation of Negroes. Similar to the KKK."

46. Dori Laub, "Bearing Witness or the Vicissitudes of Listening," *Testimony: Crisis of Witnessing in Literature, Psychoanalysis, and History,* Shoshana Felman and Dori Laub (New York: Routledge, 1992) 79.

47. Joel Williamson, *The Crucible of Race* (New York: Oxford UP, 1984) 224.

48. Hurston's depiction of John Pearson invites an examination of the relationship between plantation legacies and overly sexualized, violent definitions of manhood. *Jonah's Gourd Vine* provides an insightful cultural analysis of postbellum gender roles because it sensitively addresses gender issues in the wake of slavery.

49. Zora Neale Hurston, "Crazy for this Democracy," *Zora Neale Hurston: Folklore Memoirs and Other Writings,* ed. Cheryl Wall (New York: Library of America, 1995) 948.

50. I say "many" to acknowledge that Hurston did not write about every regional or every socio-economic group of African Americans. In spite of this, her focus on the conditions in the rural South addresses the concerns of millions. Harvard Sitkoff, *A New Deal for Blacks: The Emergence of Rights as a National Issue* (New York: Oxford UP, 1978). Even though between 1890 and 1910 nearly 200,000 Southern blacks moved North, in 1910 "more than 90 percent of African Americans lived in the South . . . three quarters of them in rural areas" (10).

51. Hortense Spillers, "All the Things You Could Be by Now, If Sigmund Freud's Wife Was Your Mother: Psychoanalysis and Race," *Female Subjects in Black and White: Race, Psychoanalysis, Feminism,* eds. Elizabeth Abel, Barbara Christian, and Helene Moglen (Berkeley: U of California P, 1997) 135.

52. Zora Neale Hurston, "Characteristics of Negro Expression," *Hurston: Folklore, Memoirs and Other Writings,* ed. Cheryl A. Wall (New York: Literary Classics, 1995) 838. The idea of transforming African Americans through education was a highly debated issue within both the black and white communities. Whereas African American leaders promoted education as a necessity for black children, many members of the white community felt that black children had limited intellectual abilities. Sadly, the publication and popularity of the best-selling work *The Bell Curve Wars: Race, Intelligence, and the Future of America,* attests to the longevity of this discussion, ed. Steven Fraser (New York: Basic Books, 1995). While Hurston valued education and was very concerned with the quality of black schools, she was equally concerned that certain types of education not destroy African American culture. She saw "the Negro [as] a very original being. While he lives and moves in the midst of a white civilization, everything that he touches is reinterpreted for his own use." She wanted this particular transforming power to remain alive within African American culture.

53. The link between freedom and education was originally forged through injunctions against teaching slaves to read and write.

54. Zora Neale Hurston, "The Rise of the Begging Joints," *Zora Neale Hurston: Folklore Memoirs and Other Writings,* ed. Cheryl Wall (New York: Library of America, 1995) 929.

55. Pamela Bordelon, ed., *Go Gator and Muddy the Water: Writings by Zora Neale Hurston from the Federal Writers' Project* (New York: W. W. Norton, 1999) 13, 14. The Federal Writers' Project was created under the umbrella of Roosevelt's Work Projects Administration to provide a source of income for artists during the Depression years. In 1938, Hurston signed on as a consultant for the publication of a study called *The Florida Negro.*

56. Zora Neale Hurston, "Art and Such," *Zora Neale Hurston: Folklore Memoirs and Other Writings,* ed. Cheryl Wall (New York: Library of America, 1995) 906. This article was originally written in 1938 while Hurston was employed by the Federal Writers' Project to gather data and help produce a state African American history, *The Florida Negro: A Federal Writers' Project Legacy.* All of her work was deleted from the project's final manuscript, which was eventually published in 1993.

57. Frederick Douglass, *Narrative of the Life of Frederick Douglass, an American Slave* (New York: W.W. Norton, 1997) 84.

58. Zora Neale Hurston, "Crazy for This Democracy," *Zora Neale Hurston: Folklore Memoirs and Other Writings,* ed. Cheryl Wall (New York: Library of America, 1995) 948.

59. Cheryl Wall, "Changing Her Own Words," *Zora Neale Hurston: Critical Perspectives Past and Present* (New York: Amistad, 1993) 86.

60. Winthrop Jordan, *The White Man's Burden: Historical Origins of Racism in the United States* (London: Oxford, UP, 1974) 79.

61. Jordan, *The White Man's Burden: Historical Origins of Racism in the United States,* 80.

62. Joel Williamson, *The Crucible of Race: Black-White Relations in the American South Since Emancipation* (New York: Oxford UP, 1984) 114.

63. Hazel Carby, "On the Threshold of the Women's Era: Lynching, Empire, and Sexuality," *Race, Writing, and Difference,* ed. Henry Louis Gates (Chicago: U of Chicago P, 1986) 117. Carby applauds Ida B. Wells for her analysis of patriarchal manipulations of gender in her 1892 pamphlet *Southern Horror: Lynch Law in All Its Phases.* The pamphlet addresses the relationship between political and economic disfranchisement and immoral behavior. Hurston's 1934 fictional representation of the same patriarchal system provides a similar analysis to the one Wells gives in the 1890s.

64. Joel Williamson, *The Crucible of Race: Black-White Relations in the American South Since Emancipation,* 116.

65. Jean Walton, "Re-Placing Race," *Female Subjects in Black and White,* eds., Elizabeth Abel, Barbara Christian, and Helene Moglen (Berkeley: U of California P, 1997) 243. Walton argues that race influences gender and that sexuality constructs in the formation of feminine identity; I suggest that this is equally true in the formation of masculine identities. Furthermore, as stated in the introduction, the oppressive functions of race, gender, and class constructs often facilitate violence and other forms of trauma.

66. Hazel Carby, "On the Threshold of Women's Era: Lynching, Empire, and Sexuality in Black Feminist Theory," *"Race," Writing, and Difference,* ed. Henry Louis Gates (Chicago: U of Chicago P, 1986) 307.

67. Carby, "On the Threshold of Women's Era: Lynching, Empire, and Sexuality in Black Feminist Theory," 315.

68. The sphere of masculine authority has been clearly redefined over that last fifty years and continues to be in flux. This reference is time and place specific.

69. Sue K. Jewell, *From Mammy to Miss America and Beyond: Cultural Images and the Shaping of U.S. Social Policy* (London: Routledge, 1993) 132.

70. Dierdre Lashgari, "To Speak the Unspeakable: Implications of Gender, 'Race,' Class, and Culture," *Violence, Silence, and Anger: Women's Writing as Transgression* (Charlottesville: UP of Virginia, 1995) 8. It is important to make clear, as Lashgari does, that "[t]here are no simple dichotomies. Men . . . have also been scarred by patriarchy. And men are not the only oppressors. Women have frequently played a role in keeping the mechanisms of patriarchy in place, as many men have worked as allies in dismantling them."

71. Frances Smith Foster, Introduction, *Witnessing Slavery* (Madison: U of Wisconsin P, 1979) xxxii.

72. Robert Hemenway's biography and Hurston's autobiography both indicate that, like the character John Pearson, John Hurston had numerous extramarital affairs and long absences from the home.

73. Pamela Bordelon, ed., *Go Gator and Muddy the Water: Writings by Zora Neale Hurston from the Federal Writers' Project* (New York: W. W. Norton, 1999) 7. Bordelon reports that John Hurston, similar to the character John Pearson, died in a car-train collision in May 1918.

74. Mary Helen Washington, "'The Darkened Eye Restored': Notes Toward a Literary History of Black Women," *Reading Black, Reading Feminist,* ed. Henry Louis Gates (New York: Penguin, 1990) 100.

Chapter 2: Gender Relations and Testimony in *Jonah's Gourd Vine*

1. Alice Walker, *In Search of Our Mothers' Gardens* (San Diego: Harcourt Brace, 1983) 13.

2. Virginia Woolf, *A Room of One's Own* (New York: Harcourt Brace, 1929) 101.

3. Lee Alfred Wright, *Identity, Family, and Folklore in African American Literature* (New York: Garland Publishing, 1995) 52, 53. Wright discusses the static images that constitute Hurston's male characters as a way of contrasting them with Alice Walker's male characters.

4. Paula Giddings, *When and Where I Enter: The Impact of Black Women on Race and Sex in America* (New York: Quill William Morrow, 1984) 64. As Giddings notes, Frances Harper was quite aware of the conditions plaguing many black women during this time. By 1870, Harper was complaining that on her tour of the South she had to spend much of her time "'preaching against men ill-treating their wives.'"

5. Barbara Smith, *The Truth That Never Hurts: Writings on Race, Gender, and Freedom* (New Brunswick: Rutgers UP, 1998) 31.

6. Shoshana Felman, "Education and Crisis," *Testimony, Crisis of Witnessing in Literature, Psycho-analysis, and History,* Shoshana Felman and Dori Laub (New York: Routledge, 1992) 46. Using the testimony of a Holocaust survivor, Felman explains the liberating and transformational potential of testimony.

7. Deirdre Lashgari, "To Speak the Unspeakable: Implications of Gender, 'Race,' Class, and Culture," *Violence, Silence and Anger: Women's Writing as Transgression* (Charlottesville: U of Virginia P, 1995) 3.

8. Jerry H. Bryant, *Victims and Heroes: Racial Violence in the African American Novel* (Amherst: U of Massachusetts P, 1997) 283. Bryant's examination of the development of a feminist theme of heroic violence demonstrates how far ahead of her time Hurston really was. Bryant notes that in literature "there was no sustained [representation of] gender antagonism before the late sixties and early seventies."

9. Lashgari, "To Speak the Unspeakable: Implications of Gender, 'Race,' Class, and Culture," 8.

10. Lashgari, "To Speak the Unspeakable: Implications of Gender, 'Race,' Class, and Culture," 8.

11. Kai Erikson, "Notes on Trauma and Community," *Trauma: Explorations in Memory,* ed. Cathy Caruth (Baltimore: Johns Hopkins UP, 1995) 185, 190.

12. Ann du Cille, *Skin Trade* (Cambridge: Harvard UP, 1996) 65.

13. du Cille, *Skin Trade* 65. Many black men worked very had to protect black women, but Hurston was concerned with those, like John, who aimed at possessing black women. Hurston's testimonial fiction speaks for the women in her family as well as the other black women who found themselves silenced in the wake of violent oppression.

14. Kevin Gaines, *Uplifting the Race: Black Leadership, Politics, and Culture in the Twentieth Century* (Chapel Hill: U of North Carolina P, 1996) 107.

15. W.E.B. Du Bois, "The Damnation of Women," *Darkwater: Voices from Within the Veil* (New York: Harcourt Brace, 1920). While he shared the Victorian ideals of his class and era, Du Bois was an outspoken defender of black women. For further reading, I suggest "The Freedom of Negro Womanhood," *The Gift of Black Folk* (1924), and numerous editorials in *Crisis* between 1910 and 1934.

16. Hazel Carby, "On the Threshold of Womens' Era: Lynching, Empire, and Sexuality on Black Feminist Theory," *'Race,' Writing, and Difference,* ed. Henry Louis Gates (Chicago: U of Chicago, 1985) 302. Carby's excellent discussion of "the intellectual discourse of black women in the 1890s" complicates the conception of male intellectual genius by examining black female intellectuals and by underscoring class differences at work in feminist discourse during the 1890s.

17. Beverly Guy-Sheftall, *Daughters of Sorrow: Black Women in United States History,* 74.

18. Gaines, *Uplifting the Race: Black Leadership, Politics, and Culture in the Twentieth Century,* 8.

19. Guy-Sheftall, *Daughters of Sorrow: Black Women in United States History,* 58.

20. Cheryl Wall, ed., Chronology, *Zora Neale Hurston: Folklore, Memoirs, and Other Writings* (New York: Penguin, 1995) 962.

21. Zora Neale Hurston, "My Most Humiliating Jim Crow Experience," *Zora Neale Hurston: Folklore Memoirs and Other Writings,* ed. Cheryl Wall, 935. The essay describing this 1931 experience was not published until June 1944 in *The Negro Digest.*

22. Amy S. Gottfried, *Historical Nightmares and Imaginative Violence in American Women's Writings* (Westwood: Greenwood Press, 1998) 9.

23. Cathy Caruth, *Unclaimed Experience: Trauma, Narrative, and History* (Baltimore: Johns Hopkins UP, 1996) 96. Caruth gives a full discussion of how trauma can produce and impose an identity upon survivors that binds them in an ethical relationship to the very event that traumatizes them. Hurston's act of testimony for her own foremothers defines her own ethical relationship to their history by ensuring that their stories are transmitted to other women.

24. Kali Tal, *Worlds of Hurt: Reading the Literatures of Trauma* (Cambridge: Cambridge UP, 1996) 9.

25. Cathy Caruth, "Recapturing the Past: Introduction," *Unclaimed Experience: Trauma, Narrative, and History* (Baltimore: Johns Hopkins UP, 1996) 156. In the closing paragraph of her introduction to this essay collection, Caruth extends the concept of a singular, consciously unassimilated traumatic experience to include those experiences that are both past and present.

26. Through *Their Eyes Were Watching God,* Hurston demonstrates that the process of testimony allows survivors to intergenerationally transmit a legacy of survival that disrupts the crippling effects of repetition associated with trauma.

27. Lee Alfred Wright, *Identity, Family, and Folklore in African American Literature* (New York: Garland, 1995) 28.

28. Wright, *Identity, Family, and Folklore in African American Literature.* For further reading, I suggest Wright's discussion of "The Good Mother Tradition"; he uses Houston Baker Jr.'s gendered reading of Harriett Jacobs's *Incidents in the Life of a Slave Girl* to examine the image of the self-sacrificing mother as a trope that appears often in African American literature, beginning with slave narratives.

29. Sally Ann Ferguson, "Folkloric Men and Female Growth in *Their Eyes Were Watching God,*" *Black American Literature Forum,* 21 (1987): 186.

30. Paula Giddings, *When and Where I Enter: The Impact of Black Women on Race and Sex in America* (New York: Quill, 1984) 75, 77. Giddings chronicles women's developing independence and response to domination through the emergence of the first black female lawyers and physicians in the 1880s, but she notes that the masses of black women were still relegated to domestic work.

31. Judith Herman, M.D., *Trauma and Recovery: The Aftermath of Violence from Domestic Abuse to Political Terror* (New York: Basic Books, 1992) 77. Herman defines patterns of dependence as one of the universal methods that perpetrators use to control their wives: "[I]n addition to inducing fear, the perpetrator seeks to destroy the victim's sense of autonomy."

32. Barbara Smith, *The Truth that Never Hurts: Writings on Race, Gender, and Freedom* (New Brunswick: Rutgers UP, 1998) 31.

33. Laura E. Tanner, *Intimate Violence: Reading Rape and Torture in Twentieth-Century Fiction* (Bloomington: Indiana UP, 1994) 3.

34. Herman, M.D., *Trauma and Recovery: The Aftermath of Violence from Domestic Abuse to Political Terror,* 77. As Herman explains, even though "violence is a universal method of terror, the perpetrator may use violence infrequently, as a last resort. It is not necessary to use violence often to keep the victim in a constant state of fear."

35. Gottfried, *Historical Nightmares and Imaginative Violence in American Women's Writings,* 11.

36. Tal, *Worlds of Hurt: Reading the Literatures of Trauma,* 121.

37. Hurston, *Jonah's Gourd Vine* (Philadelphia: Lippincott, 1934). In the glossary of terms, Hurston defines the word Cuffy as West African in origin and meaning Negro.

38. For further reading, I suggest Ann du Cille's "The Occult of True Black Womanhood: Critical Demeanor and Black Feminist Studies," *Signs: Journal of Women in Culture and Society* 19 (1994): 591–629.

39. Cheryl Wall, "Changing Her Own Words," *Zora Neale Hurston: Critical Perspectives Past and Present,* eds. Henry Louis Gates and K. A. Appiah (New York: Amistad Press, 1993) 88.

40. Robert Hemenway, *Zora Neale Hurston: A Literary Biography* (Urbana: U of Illinois P, 1977) 192. Hemenway reports that after Carl Van Vechten complained that he didn't understand the title, Hurston explained it by referring to the book of Jonah 4: 6–10. The story tells of a "prophet of God [who] sat up under a gourd vine that had grown up in one night. But a worm came along and cut it down. . . . One act of malice and it is withered and gone." Hurston condemns the

"malice" in John and Lucy's relationship by contrasting the period of courtship when Lucy "grant[s] him her special company" with John's ultimate neglect and abuse (69). While Lucy is ill, John continues his extramarital affairs and is rarely home to care for his wife and children. When Lucy chastises him, he responds violently by slapping her face. Lucy "turn[s] her face to the wall" and begins her own deathwatch (129). Their relationship culminates in Lucy's death.

41. Pamela Bordelon, ed., *Go Gator and Muddy the Water: Writings by Zora Neale Hurston from the Federal Writers' Project* (New York: W. W. Norton, 1999) 7. As mentioned in chapter 1, Bordelon reports that John Hurston died in a car-train collision in May 1918.

42. Françoise Lionnet, "Autoethnography: The An-Archic Style of Dust Tracks on a Road," *Reading Black, Reading Feminist,* ed. Henry Louis Gates (New York: Penguin 1990) 382. Lionnet's work provides insight into the origins of Hurston's persona, Isis. Lionnet notes that in her autobiography, *Dust Tracks,* Hurston "chooses Persephone as an alter ego [and] . . . the Eleusinian story of Demeter searching for Persephone has its roots in the Egyptian myth of Isis and Osiris."

43. Hemenway, *Zora Neale Hurston: A Literary Biography,* 17. Hurston was dogged in pursuit of her own education. In September 1917, she entered Morgan Academy in Baltimore, the high school division of what is now Morgan State University. While Hurston often toyed with her birth date to make herself younger, recent scholarship confirms her year of birth as 1891, making her twenty-six years old when she entered Morgan Academy. She made many sacrifices over the next ten years in order to earn a degree in anthropology from Barnard College at the age of 37.

44. Tal, *Worlds of Hurt: Reading the Literatures of Trauma,* 139.

45. Gottfried, *Historical Nightmares and Imaginative Violence in American Women's Writings,* 9–10.

Chapter 3: Testimony and Reproduction in *Their Eyes Were Watching God*

1. Henry Louis Gates, Introduction, *Reading Black, Reading Feminist,* ed. Henry Louis Gates (New York: Penguin 1990) 7.

2. Mary Helen Washington, "'The Darkened Eye Restored': Notes Toward a Literary History of Black Women," *Reading Black, Reading Feminist,* ed. Henry Louis Gates (New York: Penguin, 1990) 33.

3. Alice Walker's *The Color Purple* (1982), Gwendolyn Brooks's *Maud Martha* (1953), and Sherely Ann Williams's *Dessa Rose* (1986) are but a few examples of late twentieth-century works by black women writers whose focus on the quest for "womanness," and her correlating voice places them in direct conversation with Hurston.

4. Gwendolyn Mae Henderson, "Speaking in Tongues," *Changing Our Own Words: Essays on Criticism, Theory, and Writing by Black Women,* ed. Cheryl Wall (New Brunswick: Rutgers UP, 1989) 140.

5. Cathy Caruth, Introduction, *Trauma: Explorations in Memory,* ed. Cathy Caruth (Baltimore: Johns Hopkins UP, 1995) 11.

6. Frances Smith Foster, *Witnessing Slavery* (Madison: U of Wisconsin P, 1979) xxi.

7. Kali Tal, *Worlds of Hurt: Reading the Literatures of Trauma* (Cambridge: Cambridge UP, 1996) 127.

8. Dori Laub, "Bearing Witness or the Vicissitudes of Listening," *Testimony: Crisis of Witnessing in Literature, Psychoanalysis, and History,* Shoshana Felman and Dori Laub (New York: Routledge, 1992) 70.

9. Obeah or "magic," as practiced in Haiti, forms part of the Haitian polytheistic Voodoo religion. In an effort to trace the diasporic presence of African religious systems, Hurston set out to compare the religious practices in Jamaica and Haiti with what she found still in use among

African Americans. For further reading see Hurston's *Tell My Horse: Voodoo and Life in Haiti and Jamaica* (New York: Perennial Library, 1990).

10. Elizabeth Fox-Genovese, "My Statue, My Self: Autobiographical Writings of Afro-American Women," *Reading Black, Reading Feminist,* ed. Henry Louis Gates (New York: Penguin, 1990) 195.

11. The town of Notasulga, Alabama, is both the setting of *Jonah's Gourd Vine* and Hurston's actual birthplace. Both her parents and grandparents originate there. Chapters 1 and 2 establish the relationship between Hurston's personal testimony in *Their Eyes* and the lives of her foremothers.

12. Dori Laub, "Bearing Witness or the Vicissitudes of Listening," *Testimony: Crisis of Witnessing in Literature, Psychoanalysis, and History,* Shoshana Felman and Dori Laub (New York: Routledge, 1992) 70–71.

13. In *Jonah's Gourd Vine.* Hurston describes a similar intimacy between the fictional personas of her parents, John and Lucy Potts. See chapter 2 for a discussion of the intimate bedroom scene, which immediately follows John's use of a loaded Winchester rifle to threaten Lucy if she ever tries to leave him (111).

14. Barbara Johnson, "Thresholds of Difference: Structures of Address in Zora Neale Hurston," *Zora Neale Hurston: Critical Perspectives Past and Present,* ed. Henry Louis Gates and K. A. Appiah (New York: Amistad, 1993) 130.

15. Alice Gambrell, *Women Intellectuals, Modernism, and Difference: Transatlantic Culture, 1919–1945* (Cambridge: Cambridge UP, 1997) 13.

16. Hazel Carby, "The Politics of Fiction, Anthropology, and the Folk: Zora Neale Hurston," *History and Memory in African American Culture,* eds. Robert O'Meally and Geneviève Fabre (New York: Oxford UP, 1994) 37.

17. As a child, Hurston loved storytelling, and in *Dust Tracks,* she discusses her grandmother's desire to beat her tale-telling tendencies out of her (52–53).

18. Kali Tal, *Worlds of Hurt: Reading the Literatures of Trauma* (Cambridge: Cambridge UP, 1996) 117–118. Tal's discussion of liminality relies heavily on Eric J. Leed's discussion of it in his 1979 publication, *No Man's Land: Combat and Identity in World War I.*

19. Mary Helen Washington, "'I Love the Way Janie Crawford Left Her Husbands': Emergent Female Hero," *Zora Neale Hurston: Critical Perspectives Past and Present,* eds. Henry Louis Gates and K. A. Appiah (New York: Amistad, 1993) 101.

20. Kali Tal, *Worlds of Hurt: Reading the Literatures of Trauma* (Cambridge: Cambridge UP, 1996) 126.

21. Cathy Caruth, *Unclaimed Experience: Trauma, Narrative, and History* (Baltimore: Johns Hopkins UP, 1996) 131.

22. Caruth, *Unclaimed Experience: Trauma, Narrative, and History,* 141.

23. Dori Laub, "Bearing Witness or the Vicissitudes of Listening," *Testimony: Crisis of Witnessing in Literature, Psychoanalysis, and History,* Shoshana Felman and Dori Laub (New York: Routledge, 1992) 69.

24. Dori Laub, "Bearing Witness or the Vicissitudes of Listening," 69.

25. Dori Laub, "Bearing Witness or the Vicissitudes of Listening," 69.

26. Henry Louis Gates, "*Their Eyes Were Watching God:* Hurston and the Speakerly Text," *Zora Neale Hurston: Critical Perspectives Past and Present,* eds. Henry Louis Gates and K. A. Appiah (New York: Amistad, 1993) 188.

27. Carby, "The Politics of Fiction, Anthropology, and the Folk: Zora Neale Hurston," 39.

28. Mary Helen Washington, "'I Love the Way Janie Crawford Left Her Husbands': Emergent Female Hero," *Zora Neale Hurston: Critical Perspectives Past and Present,* eds. Henry Louis Gates and K. A. Appiah (New York: Amistad, 1993) 100.

29. See Zora Neale Hurston, letter to Dr. Grover June 15, 1932, Hurston Collection, Rare Books and Manuscripts, University of Florida Library, Gainesville, Fl. Hurston shows her affection for Eatonville in her works and also in this letter to Dr. Grover expressing her plans to put on a play and start the first "real Negro Theater." Her plans for the anticipated profits reveal her understanding of the Eatonville folk community as flawed. She says that spending money for an Eatonville "community center and some outdoor sports" would help this "I won't say immoral just unmoral town a lot."

30. Carby, "The Politics of Fiction, Anthropology, and the Folk: Zora Neale Hurston," 37.

31. Carby, "The Politics of Fiction, Anthropology, and the Folk: Zora Neale Hurston," 36.

32. For further reading, I suggest *The Power of the Porch: The Storyteller's Craft in Zora Neale Hurston, Gloria Naylor, and Randall Kenan* (Athens: U of Georgia P, 1996).

33. Harold Courlander, *A Treasury of Afro-American Folklore* (New York: Marlowe and Co., 1996) 487.

34. Pamela Bordelon, ed., *Go Gator and Muddy the Water: Writings by Zora Neale Hurston from the Federal Writers' Project* (New York: W. W. Norton, 1999) 35.

35. Zora Neale Hurston, *Dust Tracks on a Road* (Philadelphia: J. P. Lippincott, 1942) 45.

36. Zora Neale Hurston, *Dust Tracks on a Road*, 45.

37. Mary Helen Washington, "'I Love the Way Janie Crawford Left Her Husbands': Emergent Female Hero," *Zora Neale Hurston: Critical Perspectives Past and Present*, eds. Henry Louis Gates and K. A. Appiah (New York: Amistad, 1993) 102.

38. Robert Hemenway, *Zora Neale Hurston: A Literary Biography* (Urbana: U of Illinois P, 1977) 231. Hurston's lover remains unnamed, but Hemenway explains that she met A. W. P. while he was a twenty-three-year-old college student and a cast member of the 1932 production of her play, *The Great Day*. In the autobiography, *Dust Tracks*, she briefly describes the violence and intensity of their relationship.

39. Cathy Caruth, *Trauma: Explorations in Memory*, ed. Cathy Caruth (Baltimore: Johns Hopkins UP, 1995) 8.

40. Jean Chevalier and Alain Gheerbrant, *Dictionary of Symbols* (New York: Penguin, 1994) 742. Hurston's use of the pear tree as the symbolic site of perfect love reflects a despondent view in light of the symbolic definition of the pear: "In China, pear-blossom was sometimes used as a symbol of mourning because it is white but more especially as a symbol of the fleeting nature of life itself because it is so short-lived and so very easily scattered. In dreams the fruit is 'a typically erotic symbol, fraught with sensuality.'"

41. Hurston arrived in Kingston, Jamaica, on April 14, 1936, to study Obeah practices; she departed for Haiti on September 22 and began writing *Their Eyes* in October.

42. Cathy Caruth, *Unclaimed Experience: Trauma, Narrative, and History* (Baltimore: Johns Hopkins UP, 1996) 141.

43. Molly Hite, "Romance, Marginality, and Matrilineage: *The Color Purple* and *Their Eyes Were Watching God*," *Reading Black, Reading Feminist*, ed. Henry Louis Gates (New York: Penguin, 1990) 433.

44. Mary Helen Washington, "'The Darkened Eye Restored': Notes Toward a Literary History of Black Women," *Reading Black, Reading Feminist*, ed. Henry Louis Gates (New York: Penguin, 1990) 35.

45. Molly Hite, "Romance, Marginality, and Matrilineage: *The Color Purple* and *Their Eyes Were Watching God*," 447.

46. Molly Hite, "Romance, Marginality, and Matrilineage: *The Color Purple* and *Their Eyes Were Watching God*," 449.

47. In her first novel, *Jonah's Gourd Vine*, the persona of Hurston's mother, Lucy Pearson, speaks to

her daughter from her deathbed; she says, "'don' love anybody better'n you do yo'self. Do, you'll be dying befo' yo' time is out . . . uh person can be killed 'thout being struck uh blow'" (130).

48. Robert Stepto, *From Behind the Veil: A Study of Afro-American Narrative* (Urbana: U of Illinois P, 1979) 166.

Chapter 4: Sites of Rupture in *Dust Tracks on a Road*

1. Claudine Raynaud, "'Rubbing a Paragraph with a Soft Cloth: Muted Voices and Editorial Constraints in *Dust Tracks on a Road,*'" *De/Colonizing the Subject: The Politics of Gender in Women's Autobiography,* eds. Sidione Smith and Julia Watson (Minneapolis: U of Minnesota, 1992) 34–64. For further reading on the editorial constraints of this project, Raynaud engages in an interesting and in-depth discussion about the sections of *Dust Tracks* that were excised by editors from the published version. She argues that the omissions changed the structure and chronology of the text. See also Hemenway, *Zora Neale Hurston: A Literary Biography,* 275–77.
2. Robert Hemenway, *Zora Neale Hurston: A Literary Biography* (Urbana: U of Illinois P, 1977) 277.
3. Arna Bontemps, rev. of *Dust Tracks on a Road,* by Zora Neale Hurston, *New York Herald Tribune Books* November 22, 1942: 3.
4. Harold Preece, rev. of *Dust Tracks on a Road,* Zora Neale Hurston, *Tomorrow* February 3, 1943: 289. This project focuses on a trauma related testimonial reading of Hurston's work; therefore, it is important to note that harsh criticism resulting in alienation and rejection haunted Hurston's career and could be understood as another form of trauma that is linked to her drive to give testimony.
5. Harold Preece, rev. of *Their Eyes Were Watching God* by Zora Neale Hurston, *Crisis* 12 December 1936: 364, 367.
6. Alice Walker, *I Love Myself When I'm Laughing . . . And Then again When I'm Looking Mean and Impressive* (New York: The Feminist Press, 1979) 20.
7. Robert Hemenway, *Zora Neale Hurston: A Literary Biography* (Urbana: U of Illinois P, 1977) 277.
8. Hemenway, *Zora Neale Hurston: A Literary Biography,* 287.
9. Hemenway, *Zora Neale Hurston: A Literary Biography,* 286.
10. Hemenway, *Zora Neale Hurston: A Literary Biography,* 283.
11. Hemenway, *Zora Neale Hurston: A Literary Biography,* 278.
12. Alice Walker, *I Love Myself When I'm Laughing . . . And Then again When I'm Looking Mean and Impressive,* 20.
13. Hemenway, *Zora Neale Hurston: A Literary Biography,* 276.
14. Cathy Caruth, *Unclaimed Experience: Trauma, Narrative, and History* (Baltimore: Johns Hopkins UP, 1996) 5.
15. In *Seraph on the Suwanee* Hurston's protagonist, Arvay, fulfills her mother's dying wish. This scene can be read as another of Hurston's literary returns to Lucy Hurston's deathbed.
16. William L. Andrews, Introduction, *African American Autobiography: A Collection of Critical Essays* (Englewood Cliffs: Prentice Hall, 1993) 1, 2. Williams notes that in African American letters "autobiography has been recognized and celebrated since its inception as a powerful means of addressing and altering sociopolitical as well as cultural realities in the United States. . . . [Recent] interest in African American autobiography pivots on a shift from a traditional focus on the *bios* of the author, from whose example valuable insights about history and personal

conduct might be gleaned, to investigations of the *autos* and *graphe* represented in and by the text."

17. Henry Louis Gates, "Introduction on Bearing Witness," *Bearing Witness: Selections From African American Autobiography in the Twentieth Century,* ed. Henry Louis Gates (New York: Pantheon, 1991) 7, 8.

18. Gates, "Introduction on Bearing Witness," 3–9. Gates's discussion of the structure of black autobiography—the journey from object to subject—applies to the slave narratives of Harriett Jacobs, Linda Brent, and Frederick Douglass, as well as to Hurston's persona, Janie Crawford, in *Their Eyes.* Other similarities, outside of the journey from object to subject, include Janie's vague parentage, her being named Alphabet and not knowing she was black until late childhood, and the early years when she and Nanny were in a white family's care.

19. Judith Herman, M.D., *Trauma and Recovery: The Aftermath of Violence from Domestic Abuse to Political Terror* 175. Herman describes the stage of writing as the second stage of trauma recovery. She explains that in this stage, "the survivor tells the story of the trauma. She tells it completely, in depth and in detail. This work of reconstruction actually transforms the traumatic memory so that it can be integrated into the survivor's life story."

20. Zora Neale Hurston, letter to Hamilton Holt February 11, 1943, Zora Neale Hurston Papers, Hurston Collection, Rare Books and Manuscripts, University of Florida Library. Hamilton Holt was a faculty member of Rollins College in Winter Park, Florida.

21. Dori Laub, "An Event Without a Witness: Truth, Testimony and Survival," *Testimony: Crisis of Witnessing in Literature, Psychoanalysis, and History,* Shoshana Felman and Dori Laub (New York: Routledge, 1992) 79.

22. Paul de Man, "Autobiography as De-Facement." *The Rhetoric of Romanticism* (New York: Columbia UP, 1984) 69.

23. Bessel A. Van Der Kolk and Onno Van Der Hart, "The Intrusive Past: The Flexibility of Memory and the Engraving of Trauma," *Trauma: Explorations in Memory,* ed. Cathy Caruth (Baltimore: Johns Hopkins UP, 1995) 166.

24. Françoise Lionnet, "Autoethnography: The An-Archic Style of *Dust Tracks on a Road,*" *Reading Black, Reading Feminist* (New York: Penguin, 1990) 118.

25. Pamela Bordelon, ed., *Go Gator and Muddy the Water: Writings by Zora Neale Hurston from the Federal Writers' Project* (New York: W. W. Norton, 1999) 9. These difficulties explain why Hurston did not complete her high school education until she was 26 years old in Baltimore at the Morgan Academy.

26. As discussed in chapter 3, this complex notion of self-producing one's next generation may have originated with Hurston. Ralph Ellison introduces the same concept in *Invisible Man* (1952); the protagonist's journey includes a pivotal discussion with his grandfather, and his grandfather encourages him to be the producer of his own descendant. He urges the protagonist to become his own father. Because of the history of slavery and the loss of kinship that went with it, the notion of ancestry in the African American literary canon is very strong. By offering self-reproduction as a prescriptive in his novel, Ralph Ellison invites further exploration into the ways that his work may be in conversation with Hurston's.

27. Laura S. Brown, "Not Outside the Range," *Trauma: Explorations in Memory* ed. Cathy Caruth (Baltimore: Johns Hopkins UP, 1995) 102.

28. Brown, "Not Outside the Range," *Trauma: Explorations in Memory,* 107.

29. While the application to Hurston is new, I am indebted to Cathy Caruth for this insightful explanation of traumatic departure and return given in a 1997 lecture at Emory University, Atlanta, Georgia. See also Caruth's Introduction to *Trauma: Explorations in Memory* (1995) for further reading on how psychic trauma establishes competing frames of identity reference for survivors.

30. Robert Hemenway, *Zora Neale Hurston: A Literary Biography* (Urbana: U of Illinois P, 1977) 283.

31. Pamela Bordelon, ed., *Go Gator and Muddy the Water: Writings by Zora Neale Hurston from the Federal Writers' Project*, 6. According to the Hurston family Bible, Lucy Hurston died on September 19, 1909. Zora Neale Hurston was thirteen years old.

32. Sigmund Freud, *Beyond the Pleasure Principle* (1893; New York: W.W. Norton, 1989) 16.

33. The presence of psychic duality was, as previously discussed, central to the characterization of her persona, Janie Crawford, in *Their Eyes Were Watching God.*

34. Sigmund Freud, *Beyond the Pleasure Principle,* 36.

35. Dori Laub, "Truth and Testimony," *Trauma: Explorations in Memory,* ed. Cathy Caruth (Baltimore: Johns Hopkins UP, 1995) 74. Laub explains the rewounding that I refer to in his discussion of how "testimony is inherently a process of facing loss—of going through the pain of the act of witnessing."

36. Pamela Bordelon, Introduction, *Go Gator and Muddy the Water: Writings by Zora Neale Hurston from the Federal Writers' Project* (New York: W. W. Norton, 1999). Hurston often made herself younger than she was. In *Dust Tracks,* she claims to have been nine, but Bordelon's access to the Hurston family Bible establishes her age at time of her mother's death as thirteen.

37. Lawrence Langer, *Holocaust Testimonies: The Ruins of Memory* (New Haven: Yale UP, 1991) 172.

38. Cathy Caruth, *Unclaimed Experience: Trauma, Narrative, and History* (Baltimore: Johns Hopkins UP, 1996) 96. Caruth provides a full discussion of how trauma can produce and impose an identity upon survivors that binds them in an ethical relationship to the very event that traumatizes them. This ethical relationship explains Hurston's commitment to giving voice to the experiences of her foremothers.

39. Claudia Tate, *Psychoanalysis and Black Novels: Desire and the Protocols of Race* (New York: Oxford UP, 1998) 160.

40. Cathy Caruth, *Trauma: Explorations in Memory,* ed. Cathy Caruth (Baltimore: Johns Hopkins UP, 1995) 9.

41. Caruth, *Trauma: Explorations in Memory,* 9.

42. Tate, *Psychoanalysis and Black Novels: Desire and the Protocols of Race,* 160.

43. Dori Laub, "Bearing Witness or the Vicissitudes of Listening," *Testimony: Crisis of Witnessing in Literature, Psychoanalysis, and History.* Shoshana Felman and Dori Laub (New York: Routledge, 1992) 91.

44. Laub, "Bearing Witness or the Vicissitudes of Listening," *Testimony: Crisis of Witnessing in Literature, Psychoanalysis, and History,* 91.

45. Robert Hemenway, *Zora Neale Hurston: A Literary Biography* (Urbana: U of Illinois P, 1977) 277.

46. Kai Erickson, "Notes on Trauma and Community, *Trauma: Explorations in Memory,* ed. Cathy Caruth (Baltimore: Johns Hopkins, UP, 1995) 193.

Chapter 5: Hurston's Political Testimony: Trauma and Jim Crow

1. Zora Neale Hurston, "Crazy for This Democracy," *Zora Neale Hurston: Folklore Memoirs and Other Writings,* ed. Cheryl Wall (New York: Library of America, 1995) 948.

2. Even though she does not document her knowledge of this event until 1938, Hurston was very likely to have been well aware of it when it occurred. She was 29 years old in 1920.

3. Zora Neale Hurston, "Ocee Riots," *Zora Neale Hurston: Folklore Memoirs and Other Writings,* 899, 901.

4. Pamela Bordelon, ed., *Go Gator and Muddy the Water: Writings by Zora Neale Hurston from the Federal Writers' Project* (New York: W. W. Norton, 1999) 44.

5. Bordelon, *Go Gator and Muddy the Water: Writings by Zora Neale Hurston from the Federal Writers' Project,* 43.

6. Zora Neale Hurston, "My Most Humiliating Jim Crow Experience," *Zora Neale Hurston: Folklore Memoirs and Other Writings,* 935.

7. Letter from Hurston to Margrit de Sahloniere, November 6, 1956, Zora Neale Hurston Papers, Hurston Collection, Rare Books and Manuscripts, University of Florida Library, Gainesville.

8. Bordelon, *Go Gator and Muddy the Water: Writings by Zora Neale Hurston from the Federal Writers' Project,* 13–14, 35. The Federal Writers' Project was a unit of Franklin D. Roosevelt's Works Progress Administration (WPA). This government sponsored arts program operated nationwide as a part of the post-Depression federal relief effort also known as Roosevelt's "New Deal." In the South, Florida, Louisiana, and Virginia, "Negro Units" employed black writers and attempted to produce state African American histories. Only one was published during this period, *The Negro in Virginia* (1940). In October 1935, a similar branch of the program employed Hurston, the Harlem Unit of the Federal Theater Project. In 1938, she worked for the Florida Unit.

9. Robert Hemenway, *Zora Neale Hurston: A Literary Biography* (Urbana: U of Illinois P, 1977) 276.

10. Barbara Johnson, "Thresholds of Difference: Structures of Address in Zora Neale Hurston," *Zora Neale Hurston: Critical Perspective Past and Present,* eds. Henry Louis Gates and K. A. Appiah (New York: Amistad, 1993) 130–140. For further reading, I suggest Johnson's striking argument concerning the ideologically disruptive nature of Hurston's essay in terms of its attack on racial construction.

11. Zora Neale Hurston, "How It Feels to Be Colored Me," *Zora Neale Hurston: Folklore Memoirs and Other Writings,* ed. Cheryl Wall (New York: Library of America, 1995) 826, 827, 829.

12. Alain Locke to Hurston June 2, 1928, Alain Locke Papers, Moorland Spingarn Research Center, Howard University Library, Washington, D.C.

13. Locke's anthology can be described as an embodiment of the drive toward social equity in that, overall, it demands a reconciliation between American democratic ideology and democratic practices that guarantee all citizens certain rights to due process, voting privileges, fair wages, equal access to opportunity, and so forth.

14. Letter to Locke from Hurston June 14, 1928, Alain Locke Papers, Moorland Spingarn Research Center, Howard University Library, Washington, D.C.

15. The debt was incurred to publish the first (and last) issue of *Fire !!,* ed. Wallace Thurman (1926. Westport : Negro UP, 1970), a magazine aimed at the younger Negro artists. It was a joint effort between Zora Neale Hurston, Wallace Thurman, Langston Hughes.

16. Zora Neale Hurston, "What White Publishers Won't Print," *Zora Neale Hurston: Folklore Memoirs and Other Writings,* 951.

17. Zora Neale Hurston, *Dust Tracks on a Road* (Philadelphia: J. P. Lippincott, 1942) 171.

18. Ann Douglas, *Terrible Honesty: Mongrel Manhattan in the 1920s* (New York: Farrar, Strauss, and Giroux, 1995) 104.

19. Douglas, *Terrible Honesty: Mongrel Manhattan in the 1920s,* 76.

20. For further reading on Hurston's anthropological work I suggest: *Mules and Men* (1935) as well as her contributions to Nancy Cunard's *Negro: An Anthology* (1934), Pamela Bordelon, ed., *Go Gator and Muddy the Water: Writings by Zora Neale Hurston from the Federal Writers' Project* (1999), which gathers together Hurston's writings while she worked for the Federal Writers' Project, and most recently, Carla Kaplan, ed. *Every Tongue Got to Confess: Negro Folk Tales from the Gulf States* by Zora Neale Hurston (2001).

21. Zora Neale Hurston, "Characteristics of Negro Expression," *Zora Neale Hurston: Folklore Memoirs*

and Other Writings, 838. This essay originally appeared in Nancy Cunard's *Negro: An Anthology* (1934).

22. Alain Locke, rev. of *Their Eyes Were Watching God,* by Zora Neale Hurston, *Opportunity* June 7, 1938: 23.

23. Richard Wright, rev. of *Their Eyes Were Watching God,* by Zora Neale Hurston, *New Masses* October 5, 1937: 22–25.

24. Zora Neale Hurston, *Dust Tracks on a Road,* 172.

25. Alice Walker, *In Search of Our Mothers' Gardens* (San Diego: Harcourt Brace, 1983) 89.

26. Cheryl Wall, "Changing Her Own Words," *Zora Neale Hurston: Critical Perspectives Past and Present,* eds. Henry Louis Gates and K. A. Appiah (New York: Amistad Press, 1993) 76.

27. Alice Walker, *In Search of Our Mothers' Gardens,* 89.

28. Yael Danieli, ed. *International Handbook of Multigenerational Legacies of Trauma* (New York: Plenum Press, 1998) 9.

29. Alice Walker, *In Search of Our Mothers' Gardens,* 90.

30. Claudia Tate, *Psychoanalysis and Black Novels: Desire and the Protocols of Race* (New York: Oxford UP, 1998) 175.

31. Zora Neale Hurston, "Court Order Can't Make Races Mix," *Zora Neale Hurston: Folklore Memoirs and Other Writings,* ed. Cheryl Wall (New York: Library of America, 1995) 494. Hurston's March 5, 1943 letter to Countee Cullen reiterates the extent to which Hurston would go to end Jim Crow. She suggests a show of violence, believing that whites don't understand anything else. She proposes to Cullen that "a hundred Negroes killed in the streets of Washington right now could wipe out Jim Crow in the nation so far as the law is concerned. . . . For my own part, this poor body is not so precious that I would not be willing to give it up for a good cause."

32. Zora Neale Hurston, "Crazy for this Democracy," *Zora Neale Hurston: Folklore Memoirs and Other Writings,* ed. Cheryl Wall (New York: Library of America, 1995) 947.

33. Zora Neale Hurston, "Court Order Can't Make Races Mix," *Zora Neale Hurston: Folklore Memoirs and Other Writings,* ed. Cheryl Wall (New York: Library of America, 1995) 956, 958.

34. Hurston letter to Dr. Botkin, October 6, 1944, Manuscript Division Library of Congress, Washington, D.C. Dr. Botkin was a fellow folklorist and friend who directed the Florida Writers' Project and supported Hurston's work.

Bibliography

Primary Sources

Hurston, Zora Neale. *Dust Tracks on a Road*. Philadelphia: J. P. Lippincott, 1942.
———. *Jonah's Gourd Vine*. Philadelphia: J. P. Lippincott, 1934.
———. *Their Eyes Were Watching God*. Philadelphia: J. P. Lippincott, 1937.

Secondary Sources

Andrews, William L. Introduction. *African American Autobiography: A Collection of Critical Essays*. Ed. William L. Andrews. Englewood Cliffs: Prentice, 1993.

Aptheker, Herbert. *A Documentary History of the Negro People in the United States*. New York: First Carol Press, 1990.

Blassingame, John W. *Slave Testimony: Two Centuries of Letters, Speeches, Interviews, and Autobiographies*. Baton Rouge: Louisiana State UP, 1977.

Bontemps, Arna. Rev. of *Dust Tracks on a Road*, by Zora Neale Hurston. *New York Herald Tribune Books* November 22, 1942: 3.

Bordelon, Pamela. *Go Gator and Muddy the Water: Writings by Zora Neale Hurston from the Federal Writers' Project*. New York: W. W. Norton, 1999.

Breuer, Josef, and Sigmund Freud. *Studies on Hysteria*. Trans. James Strachey. 1895. New York: Basic Books, 1999.

Brock, H. R. Rev. of *Jonah's Gourd Vine*, by Zora Neale Hurston. *New York Times Book Review* November 10, 1935: 4.

Brooks, Gwendolyn. *Maud Martha*. New York: A. M. S. Press, 1974.

Brown, Laura S. "Not outside the Range." *Trauma: Explorations in Memory*. Ed. Cathy Caruth. Baltimore: Johns Hopkins UP, 1995. 100–112.

Bryant, Jerry H. *Victims and Heroes: Racial Violence in the African American Novel*. Amherst: U of Massachusetts P, 1997.

Campbell, Joseph. *A Hero with a Thousand Faces*. Princeton: Princeton UP, 1949.

Carby, Hazel V. "On the Threshold of Womens' Era: Lynching, Empire, and Sexuality in Black

Feminist Theory." Ed. Henry Louis Gates. *"Race," Writing, and Difference*. Chicago: U of Chicago P, 1986. 300–319.

———."The Politics of Fiction, Anthropology, and the Folk: Zora Neale Hurston." Eds. Geneviève Fabre, and Robert O'Meally. *History and Memory in African American Culture*. New York: Oxford UP, 1994. 28–44.

Caruth, Cathy. ed. Trauma and Experience: Introduction. *Trauma: Explorations in Memory*. Baltimore: Johns Hopkins UP, 1995. 3–12.

———. *Unclaimed Experience: Trauma, Narrative, and History*. Baltimore: Johns Hopkins UP, 19. 96.

Chamberlain, John. Rev. of *Jonah's Gourd Vine* by Zora Neale Hurston. *New York Times,* May 3, 1934: 7.

Chevalier, Jean, and John Buchanan-Brown. *Dictionary of Symbols*. London: Penguin, 1996.

Courlander, Harold. *A Treasury of Afro-American Folklore*. New York: Marlowe and Co., 1996.

Cross, William E. "Black Psychological Functioning and the Legacy of Slavery: Myths and Realities." Ed. Yael Danieli. *International Handbook of Multigenerational Legacies of Trauma*. New York: Plenum Press, 1998. 375–397.

Cunard, Nancy, ed. *Negro: An Anthology*. London: Wishart, 1934.

Danieli, Yael, ed. *International Handbook of Multigenerational Legacies of Trauma*. New York: Plenum Press, 1998.

de Man, Paul. "Autobiography as De-Facement." *The Rhetoric of Romanticism*. New York: Columbia UP, 1984. 67–81.

Dos Passos, John. *Three Soldiers*. Boston: Houghton Mifflin, 1949.

Douglas, Ann. *Terrible Honesty: Mongrel Manhattan in the 1920s*. New York: Farrar, Strauss, and Giroux, 1995.

Douglass, Frederick. *Narrative of the Life of Frederick Douglass, an American Slave*. New York: W. W. Norton, 1997.

Du Bois, W.E.B. "The Damnation of Women." *Darkwater: Voices from within the Veil*. New York: Harcourt Brace, 1920. 163–186.

———. *Darkwater: Voices from within the Veil*. New York: Harcourt Brace, 1920.

———. "The Freedom of Negro Womanhood." *Gift of Black Folk: The Negroes in the Making of America*. Boston: Stratford, 1924. 259–273.

———. *Gift of Black Folk: The Negroes in the Making of America*. Boston: Stratford, 1924.

———. *The Souls of Black Folk*. 1903. New York: First Vintage, 1990.

du Cille, Ann. "The Occult of True Black Womanhood: Critical Demeanor and Black Feminist Studies" *Signs: Journal of Women in Culture and Society* 19 (1994): 591–629.

———. *Skin Trade*. Cambridge: Harvard UP, 1996.

Duras, Marguerite. *Hiroshima Mon Amour*. New York: Grove Press, 1961.

Ellison, Ralph. *Invisible Man*. 1952. New York: Modern Library, 1992.

———. Rev. of *Their Eyes Were Watching God,* by Zora Neale Hurston. *New Masses* May 1941: 211.

Erikson, Kai. "Notes on Trauma and Community" *Trauma: Explorations in Memory*. Ed. Cathy Caruth. Baltimore: Johns Hopkins UP, 1995. 183–199.

Fanon, Franz. *Black Skin: White Masks*. New York: Grove, 1967.

Felman, Shoshana, and Dori Laub, M.D. "Education and Crisis, or the Vicissitudes of Teaching." *Testimony: Crisis of Witnessing in Literature, Psychoanalysis, and History*. Shoshana Felman and Dori Laub. M.D. New York: Routledge, 1992. 13–60.

Ferguson, Sally Ann. "Folkloric Men and Female Growth in *Their Eyes Were Watching God*." *Black American Literature Forum* 21 (1987): 185–197.

Foster, Frances Smith. Preface and Introduction. *Witnessing Slavery*. Madison: U of Wisconsin P, 1979. ix–xxviii.

Fox-Genovese, Elizabeth. "My Statue, My Self: Autobiographical Writings of Afro-American Women." *Reading Black, Reading Feminist.* Ed. Henry Louis Gates. New York: Penguin, 1990. 176–203.

Fraser, Steven, ed. *The Bell Curve Wars: Race, Intelligence, and the Future of America.* New York: Basic Books, 1995.

Freud, Sigmund. *Beyond the Pleasure Principle.* 1893. New York: W. W. Norton, 1989.

——. *Moses and Monotheism.* Trans. Katherine Jones. New York: Vintage Books, 1967.

Friedländer, Saul. "Trauma, Memory, and Transference." *Holocaust Remembrance: The Shapes of Memory.* Ed. Geoffrey Hartman. Cambridge: Blackwell, 1994. 260–283.

Gaines, Kevin K. *Uplifting the Race: Black Leadership, Politics, and Culture in the Twentieth Century.* Chapel Hill: U of North Carolina P, 1996.

Gambrell, Alice. *Women Intellectuals, Modernism, and Difference: Transatlantic Culture, 1919–1945.* Cambridge: Cambridge UP, 1997.

Gates, Henry Louis. Introduction. *Bearing Witness: Selections From African American Autobiography in the Twentieth Century.* Ed. Henry Louis Gates. New York: Pantheon, 1991. 3–9.

——. Preface. *The Classic Slave Narratives.* New York: Penguin, 1987. i–xxix.

——. Introduction. *"Race," Writing, and Difference.* Chicago: U of Chicago P, 1985. 1-20.

——. Introduction. *Reading Black, Reading Feminist.* Ed. Henry Louis Gates. New York: Penguin, 1990. 1–17.

——. *"Their Eyes Were Watching God:* Hurston and the Speakerly Text." *Zora Neale Hurston: Critical Perspectives Past and Present.* Eds. Henry Louis Gates and K. A. Appiah. New York: Amistad, 1993. 154–203.

Giddings, Paula. *When and Where I Enter: The Impact of Black Women on Race and Sex in America.* New York: Quill, 1984.

Gottfried, Amy S. *Historical Nightmares and Imaginative Violence in American Women's Writings.* Westwood: Greenwood Press, 1998.

Guy-Sheftall, Beverly. *Daughters of Sorrow: Black Women in United States History.* New York: Carlson Publishing, 1990.

Harris, Trudier. *The Power of the Porch: The Storytellers Craft in Zora Neale Hurston, Gloria Naylor, and Randall Kenan.* Athens: U of Georgia P, 1996.

Hartman, Geoffrey, ed. Introduction. *Holocaust Remembrance: The Shapes of Memory.* Cambridge: Blackwell, 1994. 1–23.

——. "Shoah and Intellectual Witness." *Partisan Review* 1 (1998): 37.

Hemenway, Robert. *Zora Neale Hurston: A Literary Biography.* Urbana: U of Illinois P, 1977.

Hemingway, Ernest. *In Our Time.* New York: Boni Liveright, 1925.

Henderson, Gwendolyn Mae. "Speaking in Tongues." *Changing Our Own Words: Essays on Criticism, Theory, and Writing by Black Women.* Ed. Cheryl A. Wall. New Brunswick: Rutgers UP, 1989. 13–37.

Henke, Suzette. *Trauma and Testimony in Women's Life Writing.* 1998. New York, St. Martin's, 2000.

Herman, Judith, M.D. *Trauma and Recovery: The Aftermath of Violence from Domestic Abuse to Political Terror.* New York: Basic Books, 1992.

Hersey, John. *Hiroshima.* New York: A.A. Knopf, 1946.

Hite, Molly. "Romance, Marginality, and Matrilineage: *The Color Purple* and *Their Eyes Were Watching God.*" *Reading Black, Reading Feminist.* Ed. Henry Louis Gates. New York: Penguin, 1990. 431–453.

hooks, bell. "Black Women: Shaping Feminist Theory." *Feminist Theory from Margin to Center.* Boston: South End Press, 1984. 1–15.

Hurston, Zora Neale. "To Alain Locke." June 14, 1928. Alain Locke Papers. Moorland Spingarn Research Center, Howard University Library, Washington, D.C.

——. "To Dr. Botkin." October 6, 1944. Manuscript Division, Library of Congress, Washington, D.C.

———. "To Countee Cullen." March 5, 1943. Alain Locke Papers. Moorland Spingarn Research Center, Howard University Library, Washington, D.C.

———. "Court Order Can't Make Races Mix." 1955. *Hurston: Folklore Memoirs and Other Writings.* Ed. Cheryl Wall. New York: Library of America, 1995. 956–958.

———."Characteristics of Negro Expression." 1934. *Hurston: Folklore Memoirs and Other Writings.* Ed. Cheryl Wall. New York: Library of America, 1995. 830–846.

———. "Crazy for This Democracy." 1945. *Hurston: Folklore Memoirs and Other Writings.* Ed. Cheryl Wall. New York: Library of America, 1995. 945–949.

———. *Every Tongue Got to Confess: Negro Folk Tales from the Gulf States.* Ed. Carla Kaplan. New York: Harper Collins, 2001.

———. "To Dr. Grover." June 15, 1932. Hurston Collection, Rare Books and Manuscripts, University of Florida Library, Gainesville.

———. "To Hamilton Holt." February 11, 1943. Zora Neale Hurston Papers, Hurston Collection, Rare Books and Manuscripts, University of Florida Library, Gainsville.

———. "How It Feels to Be Colored Me." 1928. *Hurston: Folklore Memoirs and Other Writings.* Ed. Cheryl Wall. New York: Library of America, 1995. 826–829.

———. "To Margrit de Sahloniere." November 7, 1956. Zora Neale Hurston Papers, Hurston Collection, Rare Books and Manuscripts, University of Florida Library, Gainsville.

———. *Moses, Man of the Mountain.* 1939. Urbana: U of Illinois P, 1984.

———. *Mules and Men.* Philadelphia: J. P. Lippincott, 1935.

———. "My Most Humiliating Jim Crow Experience." 1944. *Hurston: Folklore Memoirs and Other Writings.* Ed. Cheryl Wall. New York: Library of America, 1995. 935–936.

———. "The Rise of Begging Joints." 1945. *Hurston: Folklore Memoirs and Other Writings.* Ed. Cheryl Wall. New York: Library of America, 1995. 937–944.

———. *Seraph on the Suwannee.* Philadelphia: J.P. Lippincott, 1948.

———. "Spunk." *Spunk: The Selected Short Stories of Zora Neale Hurston.* Berkley: Turtle Island Foundation, 1985.

———."Sweat." *Spunk: The Selected Short Stories of Zora Neale Hurston.* Berkley: Turtle Island Foundation, 1985.

———. "Turpentine." *Go Gator and Muddy the Water: Writings by Zora Neale Hurston from the Federal Writers' Project.* Ed. Pamela Bordelon. New York: W. W. Norton, 1999. 135–137.

———. "What White Publishers Won't Print." 1950. *Hurston: Folklore Memoirs and Other Writings.* Ed. Cheryl Wall. New York: Library of America, 1995. 950–955.

Jacobs, Harriett. *Incidents in the Life of a Slave Girl.* San Diego: Harcourt Brace, 1973.

Jewell, K. Sue. *From Mammy to Miss America and Beyond: Cultural Images and the Shaping of U.S. Social Policy.* London: Routledge, 1993.

Johnson, Barbara. "Thresholds of Difference: Structures of Address in Zora Neale Hurston." *Zora Neale Hurston: Critical Perspectives Past and Present.* Ed. Henry Louis Gates and K.A. Appiah. New York: Amistad, 1993. 141–153.

Jordan, Winthrop. *The White Man's Burden: Historical Origins of Racism in the United States.* London: Oxford UP, 1974.

Langer, Lawrence. Introduction, *Holocaust Testimonies: The Ruins of Memory.* New Haven: Yale UP, 1991. i–xix.

Lashgari, Deirdre. "To Speak the Unspeakable: Implications of Gender, 'Race,' Class, and Culture." *Violence, Silence, and Anger: Womens' Writing as Transgression.* Ed. Deirdre Lashgari. Charlottesville, U of Virginia P, 1995. 1–21.

Laub, Dori. "Bearing Witness or the Vicissitudes of Listening." *Testimony: Crisis of Witnessing in*

Literature, Psychoanalysis, and History. Shoshana Felman and Dori Laub, M. D. New York: Routledge, 1992. 57–74.

———. "An Event without a Witness: Truth, Testimony and Survival." *Testimony: Crisis of Witnessing in Literature, Psychoanalysis, and History*. Shoshana Felman and Dori Laub, M. D. New York: Routledge, 1992. 75–92.

———. "Truth and Testimony." *Trauma: Explorations in Memory*. Ed. Cathy Caruth. Baltimore: Johns Hopkins UP, 1995. 61–75.

Leed, Eric J. *No Man's Land: Combat and Identity in World War I*. Cambridge: Cambridge UP, 1979.

Lewis, David Levering. *When Harlem Was in Vogue*. New York: Knopf, 1981.

Lionnet, François. "Autoethnography: The An-Archic Style of *Dust Tracks on a Road*." *Reading Black, Reading Feminist*. New York: Penguin, 1990. 382–414.

Locke, Alain, ed. *The New Negro: Voices of the Harlem Renaissance*. 1925. New York: Athenaeum, 1992.

———. Rev. of Their Eyes Were Watching God by Zora Neale Hurston. *Opportunity* June 7, 1938: 23.

———. "To Zora Neale Hurston." June 2, 1928. Alain Locke Papers. Moorland Spingarn Research Center, Howard University Library, Washington, D.C.

Marks, Donald R. "Sex Violence, and Organic Consciousness in Zora Neale Hurston's *Their Eyes Were Watching God*." *Black American Literary Forum* 19 (1985): 152–157.

McDonogh, Gary, ed. *The Florida Negro: A Federal Writers' Project Legacy*. Jackson: Mississippi UP, 1993.

Morgan, Edmund S. *American Slavery: American Freedom*. New York: W. W. Norton and Company, 1975.

Morrison, Toni. *The Bluest Eye*. New York: Holt, Rinehart, and Winston, 1970.

Neal, Larry. Introduction. *Jonah's Gourd Vine*, by Zora Neale Hurston. New York: Harper, 1972. 1–9.

O'Meally, Robert, and Geneviève Fabre. *History and Memory in African-American Culture*. Oxford: Oxford UP, 1994.

Phillips, K. J. "The Phalaris Syndrome: Alain Robbe-Grillet vs. D.M. Thomas." *Women and Violence in Literature: An Essay Collection*. Ed. Katherine Anne Ackley. New York: Garland Publishing, 1990. 175–205.

Pleck, Elizabeth. *Domestic Tyranny: The Making of American Social Policy against Family Violence from Colonial Times to the Present*. New York: Oxford UP, 1987.

Preece, Harold. Rev. of *Dust Tracks on a Road*, by Zora Neale Hurston. *Tomorrow* February 3, 1943: 289.

———. Rev. of *Their Eyes Were Watching God*, by Zora Neale Hurston. *Crisis* 43:12. December 1936: 364, 367.

Rashkin, Esther. *Family Secrets and the Psychoanalysis of Narrative*. Princeton: Princeton UP, 1992.

Raynaud, Claudine. "Rubbing a Paragraph With a Soft Cloth? Muted Voices and Editorial Constraints in *Dust Tracks on a Road*." *De/Colonizing the Subject: The Politics of Gender in Women's Autobiography*. Eds. Sidonie Smith, and Julia Watson. Minneapolis: U of Minnesota P, 1992. 34–64.

Richie, Beth E. "Battered Black Women: A Challenge for the Black Community." *Words of Fire: An Anthology of African American Feminist Thought*. Ed. Beverly Guy-Sheftall. New York: New York Press, 1995. 397–404.

Rosen, Norma. "The Second Life of Holocaust Imagery." *Accidents of Influence: Writing as a Woman and a Jew in America*. Albany: State U of New York P, 1992. 133–138.

Rosenfeld, Alvin. "Jean Améry as Witness." *Holocaust Remembrance: The Shapes of Memory*. Ed. Geoffrey Hartman. Cambridge: Blackwell, 1994. 56–73.

Shockley, Anne Allen. *Loving Her*. Boston: Northeastern UP, 1997.

Sitkoff, Harvard. *A New Deal for Blacks: The Emergence of Rights as a National Issue*. New York: Oxford UP, 1978.

Smith, Barbara. *The Truth That Never Hurts: Writings on Race, Gender, and Freedom*. New Brunswick: Rutgers UP, 1998.

Snead, James A. "Repetition as a Figure of Black Culture." *Black Literature and Literary Theory*. Ed. Henry Louis Gates. New York: Routledge, 1990. 59–79.

Spillers, Hortense. "All the Things You Could Be by Now, If Sigmund Freud's Wife Was Your Mother: Psychoanalysis and Race." *Female Subjects in Black and White: Race, Psychoanalysis, and Feminism*. Eds. Elizabeth Abel, Barbara Christian, and Helene Moglen. Berkeley: U of California P, 1997. 135–158.

Stein, Gertrude. *Wars I Have Seen*. New York: Random House, 1945.

Stepto, Robert. *From Behind the Veil: A Study of Afro-American Narrative*. Urbana: U of Illinois P, 1979.

Tal, Kali. *Worlds of Hurt: Reading the Literatures of Trauma*. Cambridge: Cambridge UP, 1996.

Tanner, Laura E. *Intimate Violence: Reading Rape and Torture in Twentieth-Century Fiction*. Bloomington: Indiana UP, 1994.

Tate, Claudia. *Psychoanalysis and Black Novels: Desire and the Protocols of Race*. New York: Oxford UP, 1998.

Thurman, Wallace, ed. *Fire!!*. 1926. Westport: Negro UP, 1970.

Van Der Kolk, Bessel A., and Onno Van Der Hart. "The Intrusive Past: The Flexibility of Memory and the Engraving of Trauma." *Trauma: Explorations in Memory*. Ed. Cathy Caruth. Baltimore: Johns Hopkins UP, 1995. 158–182.

Walker, Alice. *The Color Purple*. New York: Washington Press, 1982.

———. *I Love Myself When I'm Laughing . . . And Then Again When I'm Looking Mean and Impressive*. New York: Feminist Press, 1979.

———. *In Love and Trouble: Stories of Black Women*. New York: Harcourt, 1974.

———. "Saving the Life That Could Be Your Own." *In Search of Our Mothers' Gardens*. San Diego: Harcourt Brace, 1983. 3–14.

———. *In Search of Our Mothers' Gardens*. San Diego: Harcourt Brace, 1983.

Wall, Cheryl. "Changing Her Own Words." *Zora Neale Hurston: Critical Perspectives Past and Present*. Eds. Henry Louis Gates and K. A. Appiah. New York: Amistad Press, 1993. 76–97.

———. *Women of the Harlem Renaissance*. Bloomington: Indiana UP, 1993.

———. ed. *Zora Neale Hurston: Folklore, Memoirs, and Other Writings*. New York: Library of America, 1995.

Walton, Jean. "Re-Placing Race in (White) Psychoanalytic Discourse." *Female Subjects in Black and White: Race, Psychoanalysis, and Feminism*. Eds. Elizabeth Abel, Barbara Christina, and Helene Moglen. Berkeley: U of California P, 1997. 223–251.

Washington, Booker T. *Up from Slavery*. New York: Doubleday, 1901.

Washington, Mary Helen. "The Darkened Eye Restored: Notes Toward a Literary History of Black Women." *Reading Black, Reading Feminist*. New York: Penguin, 1990. 30–43.

———. "'I Love the Way Janie Crawford Left Her Husbands': Emergent Female Hero." *Zora Neale Hurston: Critical: Perspectives Past and Present*. Eds. Henry Louis Gates and K. A. Appiah. New York: Amistad, 1993. 98–109.

Williams, Sherley Ann. *Dessa Rose*. New York: Berkley Books, 1986.

Williamson, Joel. *The Crucible of Race: Black-White Relations in the American South Since Emancipation*. New York: Oxford UP, 1984.

Wilson, Harriett. *Our Nig*. Ed. Henry Louis Gates. New York: Vintage Press, 1983.

Woolf, Virginia. *A Room of One's Own*. New York: Harcourt Brace, 1929.

Workers of the Writers' Program of the WPA in Virginia. *The Negro in Virginia*. Winston Salem: J.F. Blair, 1994.

Wright, Alfred Lee. *Identity, Family, and Folklore in African American Literature*. New York: Garland, 1995.

Wright, Richard. *Black Boy*. Cleveland New York: World Pub, 1945.

———. *Native Son*. 1940. New York: Harper Classics, 1998.

———. Rev. of *Their Eyes Were Watching God*, by Zora Neale Hurston. *New Masses* October 5, 1937: 22–25.

Index